Kind Words For Tired Teachers:

Rediscover Your Passion And Purpose

VIVIENNE SMITH

Published in 2024 by Discover Your Bounce Publishing

www.discoveryourbouncepublishing.com

978-1-914428-32-6

Page design and typesetting by Discover Your Bounce Publishing

PRAISE FOR KIND WORDS FOR TIRED TEACHERS

"A rich collection of teacher reflections about our amazing profession and the many challenges we face alongside the best of experiences. Highly recommended."

Dame Alison Peacock DL, DLitt,

Chief Executive at Chartered College of Teaching

"...why would I read this book? Because we all love a story, to compare it to our own. We all face the same challenges, horrors and joys in teaching, yet some teachers react so differently. Sometimes we dismiss them...but at other times their idea is a perfect gift we didn't know we needed. So, come to this book for unexpected gifts and fascinating stories...Vivienne helps you apply what you've read to your own life. Change your story."

Dominic Salles

(YouTube English teacher; consultant and progress advisor to school leaders; author of multiple revision guides and education books, including "The Slightly Awesome Teacher.")

DEDICATION

I would like to dedicate this book to the teachers: those who inspired me as a student; those who generously gave their time to be interviewed for the book; those I've had the privilege to work with who became friends and mentors and whose belief in me helped to shape me into the teacher, writer and coach I am today.

ACKNOWLEDGMENTS

My heartfelt thanks go to: my friends and family, whose love and support is a daily blessing; Shaa, Matt, Steph and Kym at The Published Expert and Nicky, Mark and Sharon at Discover Your Bounce Publishing - who have all helped this book on its journey.

CONTENTS

INTRODUCTION

This book includes my own personal journey of training during the Covid-19 pandemic, battling back from the brink of burnout to discover a renewed sense of passion and purpose, and why I'm *not* a tired teacher any longer!

Morale and retention in the profession are at an all-time low and most schools don't have an HR department. The book is for teachers who feel broken: who want to stay but need help to thrive, or are tempted to leave, but wonder if there's life after teaching. It's by teachers, for teachers (those who stayed and those who left) who provide invaluable, candid advice and real-life examples. Readers will gain greater clarity about what they need to do now and confidence to take the next steps. It's also a great gift – because everyone has a tired teacher in their life!

Once upon a time in the not-too-distant past, I would have been the first to pick up a copy of this book. As a mature student taking my PGCE, then NQT, during successive lockdowns and remote teaching, then back in the secondary school classroom, tiredness defined my existence. My first thought in the morning was when I'd be able to collapse back into bed that night and my last thought at night was how early I'd have to rise the next morning. The sad fact is that I would have taken this book home intending to read it immediately, but most likely it would sit on my bedside table as an occasional treat to indulge in because I was far too busy to read anything other than GCSE texts and books on behaviour management or pedagogical practice.

It's hard for those outside the teaching profession to understand the many factors that go towards that tiredness. There are the never-ending piles of marking, data entry, progress reports, placating pushy parents, the looming – or current - Ofsted inspection and the toll that dealing with those 'repeat behaviour offenders' takes. Add to this differentiation for less able students and extra help for children who are struggling with anything from friendship woes to neglect or disruption at home due to a death or separation. Oh: and of course, we must strive to remain patient, calm and cheerful with every child and colleague (however trying) - and provide engaging lessons with just the right amount of stretch and challenge. This (by no means exhaustive) list presupposes that everything is running like clockwork at home. It needs to be - because we simply don't have sufficient bandwidth to deal with stroppy spouses, toddlers, or teenagers of our own. The onerous task of setting cover for every lesson that we miss means that it's simply not possible to be sick or have any domestic emergencies during term time and half terms are packed with medical or dental check-ups, visits to the vet, hair appointments, domestic repairs (be they physical ones such as the boiler, or emotional ones to try and reconnect with your long-suffering partner, family or friends).

On a serious note, there are teachers everywhere – kind, caring, committed to giving students the best possible experience in school and the best possible chances of progression – who feel completely broken right now. If you are one of them, or you know one of them, then this book is for you. Right now, you might be wondering how you can survive this job, or if you should find out whether there is life after teaching. Perhaps you are simply looking for some ways to thrive and flourish, rather than barely hanging on by your fingertips until half term or the holidays. If any of those descriptions ring true, then this book is for you too.

I have spoken to many teachers whilst researching and writing this book and included their stories, advice and experience along with mine. Like my readers and the teachers I coach, they represent a broad spectrum of age, experience, seniority and subject specialism. Some are still at the chalk-face and have no plans to step away; some have reached the point where they feel that this noble profession has taken its toll on their physical and mental health and are considering leaving; others – like me – have chosen to use their teaching qualifications in a way that fits more comfortably with their idea of work-life balance. All of us have stories to tell which might sound familiar, practical advice to offer and encouragement to give wherever you find yourself on that scale. We recognise you; we support you and we stand with you.

How to use this book:

To make life easier, I have given you a brief bio in Chapter One for each of the teachers featured in the book. Some were happy to be named, whilst others prefer to remain anonymous.

You will find their words of wisdom from Chapter Two onwards.

Each chapter deals with different aspects of teaching, to make it easier and more logical for you to find. If there is a particular teacher you like the sound of (or particularly want advice from), just look for their initials as you progress through the book.

I will be your guide and coach throughout the book and add my thoughts and experiences where they might resonate with you. At the end of each chapter, I have summarised the key takeaways for you and written some reflection questions. To get the best out of your reading, pause each time before moving on to the next chapter and take the time to jot down your thoughts.

CHAPTER ONE
MEET THE TEACHERS!

VIVIENNE SMITH, your author: I am a certified coach, qualified teacher, speaker and author. My life's work so far has been varied (which is exactly how I like it) and has included a stint as a local radio presenter, Personal Presentation consultant, running women's business networking clubs, writing a book for – and coaching – single mums and a job as Artist in Residence at my sons' primary school. However, there are four threads that run throughout my career and my work with children and adults and tie it all together: creativity, compassion, confidence and communication. My experiences both in (and outside of) teaching make me uniquely qualified to be your coach and guide. You can find out more about my story – and how to work with me – at the end of this book.

DOMINIC SALLES (DS) Known to his thousands of student followers on YouTube as "Mr Salles Teaches English," polymath Dominic is a former teacher; current teaching, learning and curriculum consultant and progress advisor to school leaders. He is also the author of multiple revision guides and education books, including "The Slightly Awesome Teacher."

DAME ALISON PEACOCK, DBE DL FRSA **(AP)** is the CEO of the Chartered College of Teaching. Her teaching career spans primary, secondary and advisory roles. She became one of the first women to receive honorary fellowship from Queen's College, Cambridge and is a trustee for Teach First. Alison has worked in educational research throughout her career and has contributed to many books including "Learning Without Limits." After her appointment as headteacher of Wroxham Primary School in 2003, she led the school out of special measures within a year to "outstanding" by year three. Dame Alison sat on the "Beyond Ofsted" inquiry, as part of the expert advisory board to the Education Select Committee, looking at the future of schools inspection in England.

SG is a Modern Foreign Languages (MFL) teacher and former department head and has 16 years of experience in teaching in a wide range of school settings both in the UK and abroad.

LOUISSA OSORIO-DENNEY (LOD) is a former MFL teacher and department head with experience of working in a secondary school in a deprived area of a large city, with a high proportion of school refusers and challenging student behaviour. She now works in the charity sector.

KAT PERRY (KP), previously a head of department and qualified teacher of 20 years with a wealth of experience in mainstream schools and the education sector, has worked across West Sussex for the last 10 years supporting learners with a variety of needs, including those with social, emotional and mental health challenges, as well as Special Educational Needs. Kat established **Learn With Confidence** when it became apparent there were many young people finding it difficult to access education through traditional means and looking for an alternative way to achieve academic success. The centre aims to empower families and offer them a choice in their educational path, depending on the needs of the learner

www.learnwithconfidence.co.uk

01403 586029

GP is a media teacher, vocational lead and lead examiner for a well-known exam board, whose extensive experience in a number of schools includes gap head of department, director of arts, timetable planner and head of pupil premium.

SEC is an English and Health and Social Care teacher and former Department Head, who has 20 years of teaching experience and is in the process of retiring (reluctantly) from the profession.

KIT MESSENGER (KM) (then a much-loved headteacher at a Sussex primary school) made headlines in 2016 when, after 23 years in education, she resigned from her post citing in an open letter that she had arrived at this "heartbreaking" decision due to "bureaucratic tasks which have little or no positive impact" on students, the increasing demands of a punishing workload on her staff and the then Conservative Education Department's plans to force all schools to become academies.

Kit, a Teaching Fellow at the University of Sussex, is the co-author of 'Curious Not Furious: Empowering Children to take charge of their behaviour – a practical toolkit". She is also a co-founder and director of Changing Chances, a community interest company (which exists to benefit the community, rather than shareholders), which offers training for parents, carers, schools and professionals working with children – from police officers to youth workers and therapists.
LinkedIn: Kit Messenger Educational Consultant, Trainer and Workplace Coach
www.changingchances.co.uk
'Curious Not Furious' is available on Amazon.

SMA is a form tutor and Computer Science Teacher of four years with a background of mentoring young people and extensive experience in the IT industry.

EP has worked for the past six years as a Teacher of English in a Secondary School in the Northeast of England.

JESSICA MARTIN (JM) taught Science for four years at secondary level before leaving mainstream teaching to create her online science tutoring business.
Shop www.buymeacoffee.com/wandw
Website: whiteboardsandwonders.co.uk

CHAPTER TWO
WHY I'M NOT A TIRED TEACHER ANYMORE!

If you are reading this book, I know you will agree with me that it is a great privilege to work with young people. Teaching offers variety, challenge, job satisfaction, a stimulating environment, humour and heart-warming moments. It's hard to imagine a job more rewarding or inspiring and we must hang on to that, even when it also feels like one of the hardest jobs in the world.

From the outset, I wanted to make a positive difference and when I feel I have been able to do this, it makes everything worthwhile and reminds me why I love teaching. One of the things I love most is when a shy student surprises me with a question, comment or answer which demonstrates that (even if they are reluctant to take the limelight and discuss this in front of the whole class) they have been taking everything in and this has sparked an exciting idea, answered a puzzling question or prompted the start of an inspiring burst of creativity. I also love being able to give young people coping strategies to deal with anything from crippling anxiety to low self-esteem or traumatic situations and have always sought to use my coaching skills to good effect whenever the need and opportunity arises.

These days my work with ESU (The English Speaking Union charity) gives me the chance to deliver Oracy CPD to teachers and visit a variety of primary and secondary classrooms to deliver public speaking and debating workshops to students. During a morning session with Year 6 students at a primary school in Peckham, south London recently I was blown away by a very eloquent speech by a softly spoken young man on the topic of what he would change if he ruled the world. It turned out he had been watching a TV programme with his parents about gender pay inequality, so if he ruled the world, he wanted to make sure that women got equal wages. I explained that when he grew up, he would indeed be able to do something about this. The only problem, he explained, was that he wanted to be a famous footballer. After musing about my suggestion that this would be a brilliant platform to influence changes to a fairer society, he realised that Marcus Rashford had done just that and so could he. In the roundabout way that children have of letting you know they like you, he asked if he and the class would be seeing me again…

I have the somewhat dubious honour of belonging to the PGCE cohort hardest hit by the appearance of Covid. In practical terms, this meant that our second placement was instantly cut short when the first lockdown was announced. I remember being in the staffroom and looking out of the window to see my erstwhile mentor running down the corridor, his face a picture of horrified panic. He and his colleagues were in such a state in fact, that they only remembered to inform us PGCE students as a kind of afterthought that we should pack up all our stuff, never to return! Some schools continued to give their placement students a way to help and stay involved, albeit remotely, but this did not happen in that case. We were then faced with the long hot months of lockdown trying to summon the enthusiasm and drive to complete our PGCE remotely. Vague instructions regarding 'reading widely' were issued and of course we still needed to finish those all-important assignments, but morale and energy levels were at an all-time low (along with the rest of the country) and the state of global emergency and those - sometimes daily - televised updates and directives felt far more compelling than self-directed study.

Embarking on my first fixed-term contract as an NQT in those early Covid days was quite an eye-opener. My first assembly in the sports hall was a dystopian vision which resembled a scene from The Handmaid's Tale: rows upon rows of anonymous children silently sitting cross-legged on the floor, each wearing a mask. The lovely, warm atmosphere of camaraderie within department that I remembered from my first placement had all but disappeared, only to be replaced by an attitude of extreme nervousness regarding this new and deadly infection, distancing policies which meant that not all staff could fit in the previously cosy department staffroom, and awkward conversations with surgical masks on. The decision at my school was for classes to largely stay put, which left teachers tearing across a very large school site several times a day clutching resources, laptop and sanitiser spray in the unrealistic five minutes between periods. Once in the classroom, where students were either literally or metaphorically sitting with their feet up, we then had to sanitise all desks, student hands and workstations and log in before even attempting to engage the class sufficiently to begin teaching. All this would have to be repeated at the end of each lesson too, before fighting through the crowded, Covid-spreading corridor crush, repeatedly muttering, "Put your mask on! No – not like that!" to every group of passing students.

I vividly remember glancing up during a Year 9 class to find a member of the office staff gesticulating urgently at me from outside in the corridor. When I went out to see what the problem was, she informed me that my son (who was still living at home at the time) had contracted Covid and I must therefore immediately gather my personal effects (not even waiting until the end of the lesson) and – to the bemusement of my pupils - vacate the school building until it was deemed safe to return! Controversially perhaps, I enjoyed this enforced break from the rigours of teaching. I particularly enjoyed having the time for a proper walk every morning, proper conversations with loved ones and spending some blissful and therapeutic periods in my garden. I was already feeling deeply stressed and more than a little burnt out by then, with the anxiety forever lurking at the edge - and often at the forefront - of my mind, which was to characterise my days as a full-time teacher.

What helped me reach my decision to move on from teaching (apart from the demands of being a part-time carer for my elderly mum and 18-month-old twin grandbabies) was that I got to the stage where I suspected that: in order to thrive in that environment, I would have to be a different person, to turn myself into something else. That's a very strange feeling because I just don't think that's healthy. I think you must be *you*; you're a better teacher when you're being yourself. Now I'm coaching, delivering workshops, tutoring and teaching 1:1 and loving it, because I don't need to be someone else in order to succeed at what I do.

I have always found that life comes full circle; nothing learnt is ever wasted. 10 years ago, I was able to use my experience of being a single mum to support others when I wrote my first book (*'The Single Mum's Survival Guide'*) and use my coaching skills to work with solo parents in person. Now I can put my - sometimes traumatic - journey as a teacher to good use in writing this book and act as a safe place and sounding board when I coach teachers seeking a positive transition to a happier situation. I can also help my students become more confident and express themselves more skilfully through my teaching, coaching and oracy work.

Vivienne's KEY TAKEAWAYS

Teaching brings both rewards and challenges. The pandemic affected not just students, but a generation of trainee teachers, as well as changing relationships between colleagues in schools across the country. It's important to inhabit a space in your working life where you can be your true self. Even if you choose a different career trajectory, you can still utilise all your unique qualities and the skills you've acquired in that new setting; nothing is ever wasted.

Reflection QUESTIONS

1. What has been your biggest challenge in teaching?

_____

_____

_____

_____

_____

_____

2. Which aspects of your teaching practice do you find most rewarding?

_____

_____

_____

_____

_____

_____

CHAPTER THREE
HOW DID IT ALL START?

DS

I moved to Ibiza when I was three and then left when I was 10. My parents were free thinkers. They didn't really think about the consequences or the future, which was fantastic because they would try anything. But it also meant they didn't protect themselves against disaster. When I was 10, we had to leave Ibiza because my dad had gambled away two businesses and the two flats they owned and the heavy mob just turned up outside the flat we were living in and said, "You've got a week to get out. We own the deeds to your flat." My dad had at this point mysteriously disappeared... My mum's Canadian friend said, "Come over, we'll put you up for a bit." So, we went off to Canada and became illegal immigrants. We were only there for ten months, and we lived in loads of different places.

Eventually my dad mysteriously arrived back on the scene and my parents decided they couldn't make a life as illegal immigrants in Canada and asked to be deported back to the UK. We started from nothing as homeless people in Camden. We lived next door to Euston station in a bed and breakfast hotel for what was then the record of 17 months (it's probably much worse now). And they just started from scratch again - from zero. The great thing about that as an upbringing is that it teaches you that you can overcome most disasters, and I kind of thank them for that.

I had a job as a tax inspector; I blame my wife for that! I had what was considered a massive overdraft of £1000 after I finished university and my wife (who was a year ahead of me and already settled) said, "Well, I'm not going to look after you, you know!" She sent me this advert for the Inland Revenue and if you went on the graduate recruitment scheme, they promised to put you wherever you wanted in the country, so I was guaranteed a job in Swindon. I applied and to this day, I'm convinced they took me on as a kind of bizarre test case of their system. There was a two-day intensive set of psychological tests, group work, IQ, all sorts of things. Two solid days. And it was just me and loads of people from Oxford and Cambridge Uni and I rocked up in my polyester suit, knowing nothing!

Amazingly, they recruited me – and they'd made the process so difficult that I thought this must be awesome, I've got to take the job! It was a terrible mistake. I was good at the investigation side of being a tax inspector - I was like a super detective and that aspect of the job I loved. It's all the tactical stuff that I just couldn't be bothered with. But strangely, I've taken that into my role in schools because my superpower (if I've got one) is looking at data and working out what the real story is behind it because schools are full of people citing data and coming to ridiculous conclusions about it that make absolutely no sense! That's the kind of skill that's lasted. But the rest of the job was soul destroying.

I've taught English for 30 years and now I've got what's called a portfolio career. If we break my time up: until January, I was four days a week in different schools. They ring me up if they're given an Ofsted ruling of "inadequate" or "requires improvement" and then I come in and I do my thing with the data. I say, "This is really important. Let's do that. Let's not bother with that - it looks important but isn't. Let me tell you why…" I only work with schools on an ongoing basis. In the run up to exam season, I'm in schools perhaps one day a week. The rest is devoted to YouTube and writing revision guides. And occasionally, when I've got a real bee in my bonnet, I'll write an education book. I do what motivates me, so the time is easy to find.

When I was teaching full time, I'd make videos for the kids I was teaching and I would think, "Well, I've got a class of 30. There's no way I can give them the individual attention they need but I can put my best explanations into a 10-to-20-minute video to help improve their grades. It was like lesson preparation. In those days I was just screen recording. I'd put my PowerPoint slides up and talk over them and a 20-minute video would probably take 30 minutes to edit and film in total. You can always find time in a weekend, especially if you know there are kids in your class who are going to watch it. There are loads of other people on the Internet watching videos, there's an added motivational factor.

AP

My motivation for going into teaching was partly: could I create a classroom where children wanted to learn? I trained in 1982 and I started in a secondary school. Then I moved to another big secondary school. After that, it was a big community college and then I moved into the advisory service, then went on maternity leave. Once we'd had our children, I went back into primary and then became a headteacher.

I've loved it wherever I've been teaching, whichever age range I've taught in, I've always thought "This is the best!" And then I've moved to something else and thought, "This is the best!"

When teaching in the secondary my sense of humour was better understood. I've always taught with a bit of humour. I think that's part of being a great teacher. Working 1:1 with children with severe learning difficulties is probably the most challenging thing I've done, because you can't really use humour in the same way.

It was energising to be part of a community of young people, e.g. when they were doing their shows at the end of the year. There was a great sense of opportunity. They're just full of life, even if they're acting out. But equally, I loved teaching the little ones, particularly early years; I had a class of 17 children that ranged between three and seven - a nice challenge. Then I taught Year 5-6, so I taught vertical group classes in a primary school and then I became a head of a primary school. The essence of great teaching is that it's not about what's 'wrong' with the child, it's about finding a way through to connect with them.

When I was a head, I could walk around my school and in half an hour take the temperature and know what was going on. If you don't know what's happening and if you don't know how your school's running, then you're becoming an administrator and you're not there to support your staff when something happens. When parents want to come and complain or ask about what's going on, how do you know if you haven't been involved?

There are various ways in which I was able to take my school from special measures to outstanding. I said we were going to become a listening school. I told all the children and the staff that we were all going to be listening to each other. It wasn't about some sort of superhero coming in with cape and tights and sorting it all out. It was very much a collective endeavour. They'd had a history of things being so bad that the only way was up. We were going to improve or be closed, so there was a real sense of: "we're all in this together and it's not about blame. This is not about deficit. This is about how this school's going to be amazing and we're going to be on this fantastic journey. Let's just get on with it." It was an incredibly positive, can-do culture.

Instead of monitoring classrooms, I was coaching much more. I'd go and sit on the table in someone's class at the end of the day and just say, "How was it today? How did Johnny get on today?" (because Johnny had a history of kicking off). Teachers are always keen to talk about children they are worrying about. Also, it's much less personal if someone's saying to you, "What else could we do to help Johnny learn?" That's much less close to the bone than saying, "What could you do differently that would mean he would sit up straight?" I needed to find a way through to understand what was going on with Johnny and then check in, so I'd say, "Did you try that? How did it go?" Teachers need to be teachers. I never once said, "Stand aside. I'll show you how to do it," or, "Oh dear. Are you doing it all wrong? Let me show you." It was how we could find a way.

For example, there was a Year 4 teacher who said, "The children in this class can't write - they've got no imagination." Instead of saying,

"Well, that's because you're shutting them down before they even started" I said, "Well, what could we do about that?" He said they were supposed to be writing about fairy tales and they were going to do something on Robin Hood. So, I replied, "Why don't you organise a Robin Hood day? The children could all make bows and arrows, and they could cook over a fire and experience being like Robin Hood and then maybe they'll be able to write about it…" I made sure that all the risk assessments were in place and that they weren't going to set fire to anything or shoot each other. I put a letter in the register that morning saying, "Dear Year 4. I hear that you're going to all be Robin Hood and his merry men today and it's going to be amazing. I can't wait to see what you're going to write about!" That teacher really led that day and came in at the end of the day glowing, because he'd had such a good day. It was his success - that was important. I wasn't crowing, "I told you you could do it!" The key was: how can I find a way through to help this teacher so that he can then help his children?

There are lots of things like that you could do to support a teacher who is finding it hard to know what to do next. It's all about enabling as opposed to judging and finding people out. The last thing that school needed was more people being found out and tripping up in the classroom. They all needed to be encouraged.

That's why I think the work I do now at the Chartered College is worthwhile because it's about encouraging the profession at scale to learn from each other to be able to appreciate success, to see that there's not just one way of doing things, but there are examples of different ways of working and the notion of collegiality and learning from each other, sharing practice and building expertise. The more we

KIND WORDS FOR TIRED TEACHERS

do that, the more our teachers are left feeling confident and inspired, the more likely it is that the children get a great deal in the classroom.

SG

I started to teach by tutoring kids at university. Then I went to America, joined a company teaching French as a foreign language to Americans and ended up with my own language school over there for a while before returning to France and working as a teaching assistant (TA) in a primary school. Afterwards I taught in college, the French equivalent of secondary school. I went back to university to do another Master's, with more linguistics. I was recruited by an organisation looking for French native speakers to take their PGCE in England. After graduating in 2008 I've taught in a wide range of schools and with a wide range of methods - private schools, Catholic schools, mainstream…

I was head of an MFL department for six years, accountable for the department and all the statistical analysis. There is no AI help with this! It's all down to you and your calculator or spreadsheet, your colour coding to see the patterns etc. That is the data part of it. But there is also creating the schemes of work, for example, in order to lead your department according to what the curriculum dictates. You are also responsible for making sure the work is implemented by doing observations, writing up reports and organising all the exams… In MFL you want to think about how you provide extracurricular enrichment for the students - the trips, clubs, competitions, etc. If a teacher in your department cannot deal with an issue with parents, you'll have to step in. When I arrived, there was no curriculum. I had to create everything from scratch, which was good in a way because I did it my way.

But I was getting home every day at seven o'clock. I was so stressed. Countless meetings with the subject leader, my line manager. I had to report the results and if they were not as expected, I had to explain why to people who didn't understand my subject and wouldn't accept any mitigating circumstances, or let me explain what the cause might be, so as to find the best solution – I was told I was making excuses! You spend your life in meetings, but you need the time to create, analyse the bigger picture – and teach, of course! I was a form tutor as well. I felt like a superhero! At least I had a personal goal, which was to make an impact, test myself and leave the department in the best possible state. When I left, the whole department had a 100% pass rate.

However, I was ruining my relationship with my partner. I was working every weekend, all the holidays. He was lovely and really supportive, but we argued often and, in the end, he said, "I can't do this. I didn't sign up for this," and he was right. I agreed it would be my last year as department head and I have never regretted it.

Now I'm part of a department rather than head of department. We all do our bit - we all have our strengths. Mine is planning. Because I did this master linguistics qualification, I like to see how the language works. I see the whole picture and I can create highly effective knowledge organisers and make sure that we are adapting the curriculum properly for the new GCSE. I love it and it takes me much less time than it would my head of department, because of my experience.

I always tell the kids that I don't need children of my own because of all the children I teach. I guess I'm still a bit of a child inside as well:

I love having a laugh when they come and tell me stories about their friendship or who they're in love with. I have a Year 7 class who are really immature. They come to class with all their little toys, and it reminds me so much of when I was a kid. Childhood is not gone. It's still there and we have such fun together!

LOD

I taught at secondary level for three and a half years. I went into teaching when I was fresh out of uni and unsure what I really wanted to do. Being a teacher was never a lifelong ambition of mine. It just happened that at the time there was a shortage of MFL teachers, and they were offering quite a handsome bursary to train. Seeing as I have Spanish, so I'm bilingual, I thought, why not just open this door? I applied to university, got a place on the course, and really enjoyed it as the PGCE progressed.

I would say there's a bit of a split as to why people go into teaching. Some are like me - they don't really know what they want to do in life, so they give it a go because there are so many teaching jobs available. Others are just born to teach, and it's been their dream, their vocation.

I taught in a large, mixed, comprehensive state secondary in a deprived area. That kind of demographic brought huge challenges, including a disdain for going to school, let alone learning languages! My first year as a classroom teacher was the first Covid year. I was given four Year 9 classes. Year 9 is always a tricky year in languages, especially if they know they are not going to continue. Two out of the four classes had 20 students out of 24 with special needs. Once, I remember looking at my Fitbit and seeing that I'd burned 4,000 calories that day.

It was because my heart was going so fast all day, every day, because of the levels of anxiety - not to mention running around the school site between bubbles. I knew I couldn't sustain it.

I often say that my last day of teaching was one of the hardest days in my life. I was just crying with all the lovely kids that I'd met who had become a vital part of my life. I thought about the bond we'd formed and what it meant to them, but also what it meant to me to make a difference to their lives. I also loved my colleagues. The staff room was raucous and lively (when we had the time to go there) with an incredible sense of camaraderie. I'm still friends with ex-colleagues, and we meet up regularly. It was a great experience to be surrounded by amazing people with a common goal.

KP

I started my career in teaching 20 years ago – not the PGCE route, but a graduate training programme where I learnt on the job and then had a day release every week to do university stuff. I did an archaeology degree. Although history is my preferred subject, I have QTS (Qualified Teacher Status) in humanities, which means I am qualified to teach geography, history and citizenship studies.

I was in a co-ed comprehensive school, which originally had about 1,100 students and included a sixth form. The school offered humanities as a core subject. I was promoted to Head of Humanities after a couple of years' teaching.

I went into teaching because I had an epiphany one day and decided that's what I wanted. I didn't have a family then. I didn't find it a problem managing the workload because I get bored really easily, and wanted something to do with my spare time in the evenings. I was there for about 11 years. For the first 10 years we were a close-knit family in our department. We were always fully supported, had such lovely relationships with all the other teachers and it didn't feel like a slog. We felt part of something important and lots of our students enjoyed spending time in our department. We had lesson plans, schemes of work, relevant worksheets and books. You adapted the resources to your class if you needed to spend more or less time on a particular topic. We had a lot more autonomy over what we were doing but if we needed help, we just had to ask. There was more freedom than perhaps some schools and teachers have today.

The decision to leave mainstream teaching was both hard, and easy. I had a child, and my priorities totally changed. My partner left at six in the morning and came back at seven at night. Most of my wages went on childcare. I took a year off on maternity leave which I found tough, to be perfectly honest - going from an ordered, organised routine to a small person that requires your constant attention but doesn't tell you what they need. Like many young people who have babies, I had high expectations. I'd been successful in my career. Why couldn't I have a child on my terms? That's how I felt, somewhat naively, when I went back to work. I thought it would be the same as it was previously which, of course, it wasn't - for numerous reasons. The school itself had changed; there'd been shifting behaviour issues and attitudes within the school, and it didn't feel like the same place. Three days after returning from maternity leave, Ofsted came in and we were put into special measures. That was a real struggle for everyone. Accountability had changed whereby, if a child didn't meet targets in terms of academic attainment, it was the teacher's fault. Nobody said, "let's look at root causes why this child isn't performing, because you're clearly doing your job."

Having a newborn, the changing shift in behaviour, an unpopular new headteacher and then being placed in special measures - it all just came together in a cacophony of noise. Something had to give. I couldn't give the baby back and I didn't particularly want to get rid of the husband, so the only other option really was for me to leave work to try and sort out things that at the time were more important. It's a shame - I'd loved teaching in that school and department - but I recognised it was something I was no longer able to manage effectively.

Schools are in desperate need of change. Leadership must be solid and collaborative to be successful and effective all the way through a school. If you have a poor leader, how can this be a successful educational establishment? I have recently discovered that this particular headteacher (who had sent a previously good school into special measures), was moved on and would not be offered any other leadership positions. It made me – and many others - feel vindicated, but it made the school a difficult place to work in and we all had to suffer.

We moved down to Sussex. I discovered I was pregnant with my second child when I handed in my notice, so I wasn't really working. I set myself up as a private tutor just to get some extra income, and I did quite a lot of moderating and a bit of exam marking, which initially I had to fit into the evenings because the kids were little, and I was a parent during the daytime. It took me about seven years to "de-school" myself. For the first three or four years I was mainly doing evening and weekend work supporting young people at school. A growing number of parents in our local area were withdrawing children from school because of anxiety or neurodiversity. Children's needs weren't being met and it was making them ill. So, parents had decided to withdraw from school, but still wanted a more organised, professional stance on education, rather than homeschooling. I ended up working with families during the day as time went on and my children started to go to nursery and school (something you wouldn't normally expect to do as a tutor). One family wanted help for their child to do GCSE history. Very quickly, I picked up other students who'd chosen or been forced into home education. I really enjoyed meeting all these diverse, interesting young people. They wouldn't necessarily fit into the school mould but were fascinating to work with and full of ideas.

'Learn with Confidence' was established officially in December 2020. My neighbour - who was also a teacher - had space free to use during the day. In the first six months we only had a few students. But we knew a number of teachers and could offer a variety of subjects - English, science, maths, the humanities. These were privately funded families, rather than through the council. It was hard to get onto the West Sussex register. Many councils support young people with EHCPs and there is a rigorous commissioning process to go through. I spent about a year working through all that paperwork. It changes constantly but I reckon we're probably working with 55 to 60 young people and their families. Not all students receive funding through EHCPs. Some come directly from local schools with funding, and others are funded by families.

Some students are only with us one hour per week, whereas others do 14. We try to combine privacy with a friendly, open plan feel, which is an interesting mix. We don't always get it right, but the key thing is collaboration with the young person and family to understand what they want regarding education, and how they work best. We don't have any groups that have educational lessons together because our learners sometimes have such spiky profiles and such different needs. The primary focus must be on meeting the needs of the individual.

Many of our parents had to give up work to support their children through their academic experience and wellbeing. We probably end up with a non-representational selection of families because these parents have had the drive, determination and desire for their children to be successful and done something about it. Getting an EHCP for a young person is hard work. There are so many hoops to jump through, and then you can't always get one, although you can appeal. I'm against a dictatorial process - You must do English, and you must do maths, and join that class. That dictatorial system wasn't meeting their needs. It's all about collaboration and autonomy.

The number of teachers at the centre is constantly changing. We have about four or five that access the centre and there are another seven or eight that are online only, dotted around the country, although a lot of our students don't necessarily want to do online. It's difficult to find local teachers in certain subjects but if a family asks for one of those subjects, I will always try to find someone through my contacts who can embrace the ethos of what we're doing. I'd love to have some local physics teachers, as well as computer science (or any science), maths…but the whole nation is having an issue with the recruitment of teachers, aren't they?

As adults, I think we can learn from young people because they're not stupid, they're observant, and they have great ideas that make you feel hopeful for our future. In subjects that I've taught, young people have risen to the challenge of understanding why things happen and how it impacts our society now, making links between current day and past events.

It's hard to look beyond the idea of education just being in a school. But once you start talking to people… teachers are all about relationships. We love to connect, and we don't get the time or energy to do that under normal circumstances. I'm certainly very excited about helping to build a community of people who started out as teachers, and now are teachers with a difference. We have a wealth of wisdom, humour, kindness and creativity. I don't think anyone really understands teaching or online teaching like teachers or ex-teachers - it's a very distinctive world. There's a sense of loneliness, a feeling that no one really gets why you're tired or stressed because of the time of year, or whatever. I see a lovely recognition and understanding amongst this group of teachers, which is quite unique.

GP

At school I was inspired by three incredible teachers who generally set out the standards for teaching for me. My English teacher Miss Kelly, my biology teacher Mrs Wilson and my drama teacher Mr Goodwin. All of them had such a love for learning and inspiring others and I could see this passion was intensified each time they found a learner that loved progressing. After university and a few years exploring my options in the dizzy world of media and broadcasting I could not shake the one passion I think I'd always had! I decided that the corporate world was not for me and in 2006 went back to the school I had left six years earlier and asked for their help to find my route.

Most teachers are inspired by those teachers that have passion for their subject and determination to help you progress. If you ask the vast majority of teachers, they have some examples of both good and bad teachers who inspired them. We go into teaching to continue giving back and inspiring future educators.

I love enthusiastic learners whose eyes physically or metaphorically widen at their own development, or when they learn something new! I love the incredible ways you can find creative ways to teach new concepts and most of all I love it when a student has done well and recognises this in themselves!

I started my teaching career in a faith school in West Sussex and as I completed training, I was lucky enough to be offered a permanent role. At the end of my NQT (Newly Qualified Teacher) year I also secured the head of department role and stayed there for 10 incredible years. I launched a yearly international trip to San Francisco and Hollywood, oversaw the integration of an Apple Regional Training Centre and spent time as part of the teaching and learning team, assistant to the timetabler and lead for DofE (Duke of Edinburgh award) Bronze.

Outside of this job I started my examining career for GCSE and have worked my way up through that organisation as a second job. I was involved in the new specification developments in 2016, including sitting on a panel for changing the content, delivering CPD around the country and designing resources for teachers and students.

Eventually, I decided I needed to spread my wings and experience another educational setting. I secured a role at an arts college in Elstree, north London/Hertfordshire, where the focus was on 14-19 and the creative sectors. I felt very at home here and within six months I became an associate senior leader, head of sixth form and then head of timetabling. Changes in my personal development really impacted me here and after some soul searching, I decided I needed to take a break from teaching. I LOVED this job, but finding myself was too important, so in 2019 I started a job in digital mental health as a remote worker and while this was amazing, nobody saw what 2020 was about to bring us.

A year into the pandemic I had achieved so much with this new job, had really found space to develop personally, and started considering what would be right for me next. My head was turned by a bit of headhunting, and at the time it seemed too good to be true. Sadly, it was - and still is - my worst experience in teaching.

As a director of arts I led nine subjects and 11 staff in a particularly challenging school. It was my first experience of a lack of support from above and unrealistic expectations. I tried very hard to focus on the students and the team but within six months I found the commute and toxic leadership too much and decided to resign. It taught me so much, both good and bad, but the reason I left teaching in 2019 was to focus on myself and there was a risk I was losing this strength.

At the same point, two great things happened: the exam board role was developing well and a chance email to a local school resulted in a job interview for a maternity cover. In January 2022 I started in a faith school as acting head of department and with a reduced commute and great developments in my personal life I had an amazing 20 months. I built some great relationships at this school and soon become a timetabler again and then took on a position as head of pupil premium for the whole school. Despite the positives, the opportunities to teach a full timetable in my subject were quickly diminishing and I felt it was right to stretch my wings once more.

In September 2023 I started as a media teacher and vocational lead at a local independent school, with a full media timetable and lots of great opportunities to get involved in the full life of the school. I am starting to find balance once again with all aspects of my career and personal life. I feel settled and I currently have two focus points - a wedding and my pension! I want to make sure that beyond teaching I am comfortable, so I am going to work hard on this over the next five years. I will only look for higher positions of responsibility if it will not impact my current way of life and living.

SEC

This will be my 20th year of teaching; I came in from the banking industry. I think I'd always wanted to be a teacher, but the funding wasn't available when I moved areas after university, so I didn't do it immediately. After my divorce, I thought, "this is what I want to do and I'm going to do it now." I have never regretted that decision. I have never, ever felt that I don't want to go into work - even on a Sunday night, even in the last five years where there have been significant points of stress in the entire industry. I'm retiring very slowly, which will end up being past the standard retirement age because I still enjoy the actual teaching.

The change for me in the last two years has been getting rid of the head of department role, which I didn't realise was so significantly draining. The stress and remuneration reward balance was shockingly bad - when I worked it out, I would actually be earning under minimum wage for the hours I do on that associated level! When I stopped, it was like getting better and only then realising how ill you were! I was teaching health and social care but also was doing quite a lot with Key Stage Five English as well. I even had to step into media at one point. Once you have that level of experience of the marking and the understanding of examination board requirements, you do it more effectively and speedily, with less stress. Whereas for teachers coming to the profession, I think what's tough is understanding the spec and understanding what the requirements are - those hoops you have to jump through, particularly in the vocational subjects. It's almost unmanageable at first and you think you're never going to understand it, but eventually you do.

SMA

This is my fourth academic year. Having industry experience in IT, I wanted to share some of that - with girls especially, as it is a kind of male dominated field. I spent a good 15 years working with men – usually with 10 other engineers where I was the only female. I had a lot of favourable comments about the way I think and work, the way I approached and communicated with clients. I used to break down the technical language in layman's terms in the way they could understand it. I updated them about what I was doing so that if I was off duty, they could hand it on to someone else to handle in my absence. With all that in mind, I felt that I wanted to share my knowledge, and I decided to go into teaching. It was about the same time that STEM became popular, and they were trying to encourage young girls to code, which I felt that I could help with.

A lot of what I love about teaching is supporting young people and seeing them succeed. Before going to teaching, I gave a lot of support to young people, especially at my church. Not just at church though – any young person that comes my way, I just want them to be successful. Also, where I have failed or made mistakes, I feel like I can encourage people to learn from that and impact their lives positively. I wanted to help students grow their skills and abilities and choose a successful career path. I knew that through teaching I would meet a lot of young people who were choosing their A-levels or planning a career.

EP

I had a placement to a sixth form college when I was training, which I loved. The obligatory bits in primary school convinced me that I had made the right choice not to teach primary, though. They were so adorable but so sticky all the time and they kept running to sit on my knee! My whole family are teachers. I wasn't actively avoiding it, but it wasn't on my radar because I had other things I wanted to do, and it wasn't until I was 28 that I started teaching. My husband had been a teacher for a couple of years beforehand. At work I didn't feel like I was doing anything to make a difference, as I wanted to. He said, "Well, why don't you do some teacher training? There's a bursary, so you won't be losing any money at least and you know the fees. You'll have an extra qualification at the end of it and if you don't like it, you don't need to do it."

I did the schools experience programme first, where you shadow teachers and get some hours of experience. It was useful to see different school settings and the different ways in which things are managed. The second one I went to was meant to be a day, but they called me back for a week. I was allowed to do what was meant to be a five-minute starter but ended up being 15! Being in front of a class teaching was electrifying. I loved it: teaching was its own sort of magic. And I thought, "This is what I'm meant to be doing!"

I think the reason most people go into teaching is very closely related to their own experiences of education, to rectify something that didn't go right when they were at school or because they had a teacher who made a big difference, who did something that positively changed their own life and they want to pay it forward. Also, some of us just really like having a captive audience – a kind of stand-up routine! As a child I was the kid wandering around telling everybody facts that I'd learned - whether they wanted to know or not! So, there's the performative side of it.

My reason for staying in teaching has a lot to do with the fact that I love my subject area. I love teaching English and getting nerdy about it. Because I love my subject area so much the national curriculum upsets me a great deal, but the bit that I get very excited about (outside of when one of the kids comes out with some very insightful analysis of a poem, or whatever) is where I've made a difference to one person; it doesn't happen that often; it doesn't happen every lesson, or with every class. I was very ill when I was at school during my exams, but I had two or three teachers who went above and beyond. One of them hand wrote notes on all the lessons I'd missed and posted them to me. That may have made a big difference to how well I performed in the exam for that subject, but it was also the fact that they hadn't forgotten me. That's the part of the job I really love.

JM

During my biology degree, I often teamed up with study buddies, bouncing ideas around and naturally taking on a bit of a teaching role. This experience, along with my time as a swimming teacher, confirmed my passion for teaching, so I went straight into my PGCE after graduating. I fell very gracefully into that. It was the right thing for me to do. I'm a confident woman, and I think I have that sort of face and that sort of personality where people come and ask me for help with things. I completed that in 2019, landed my first teaching job right away, and spent three years at that school. By the time I left in the summer of 2022, I had already been tutoring alongside my full-time job for a year. I had given my notice around Easter, knowing I was ready to transition into tutoring full-time.

There was a real tipping point. I taught one lovely lad at his house. We focused on physics because that's what he needed for his college course. When he got his GCSE results, I FaceTimed him and his family to find out how he had done in his exams, and we were just screaming at each other with pure unbridled joy. He was aiming for a Grade 8, but he ended up with a Grade 9! That really lit a fire under me.

My teaching has come on in leaps and bounds. I have never been so knowledgeable about the specification as I am now, because I have the time to really commit myself to it, to really sink my teeth in, and to know it back to front, upside down, inside out. It's incredible. When I look back, I thank God they told me I was a good teacher, but now I know how much better I am.

I finished in-person tutoring last summer. I was working for a while for my local council with children in care, care leavers and school refusers. Now I get to cherry-pick into my specialism, which only promotes better teaching. There is the flexibility to tailor lessons to a particular student. I teach groups online and I do one-to-ones as well. But my teaching style varies across my different students and my groups, just to fit the personality of the student as well as their ability, their skills and what they need to work on the most.

I only teach three days a week now, so the other two days are my admin days when I plan sessions, mark students' work, post on social media, organise my calendar and catch up with correspondence. You spin a lot of plates as a business owner, but around five o'clock (sometimes later in exam season), I have this satisfying clocking off ritual and then I'm done for the day.

Before, I had a never-ending list of things I could be doing. Now I have two separate to-do lists. They're very simple - those sticky note things on your computer screen. One is for things that need to be done this week. Maybe it's a worksheet for a student that's struggling with something specific, or writing a bespoke lesson. Those need to be done by a certain time, because the customer is expecting that. Then I have my hopeful list. I prioritise the essentials list and then pick and choose from the other, because I've met the minimum requirements for this week. If my mum calls and says, "My meeting on Friday's been cancelled. Do you want to go for breakfast?" I make sure that I am there with her, ordering my favourite Eggs Benedict.

I have recovered from the teaching trauma a bit more now and fully let go of that awful, persistent feeling that I need to be working an 80-hour week. Now I'm keeping up with housework. My house stays tidy and it's not that difficult at all! Sometimes I feel almost guilty, having left my job almost two years ago. I'm still not over having my entire weekend to myself and when I have a week off, I can do nothing related to work if I want to. But it's taken me a long time to let myself be okay with the work-life balance.

I supplement my teaching with passive income. I have two online shops. I sell resources to teachers on TES, and I also have a "Buy Me a Coffee" shop. It's a free platform for me to list digital downloads. I put things on there for students, parents and home-educated families. Now, that is a never-ending job list. I just chip away at it when I have a spare moment. This morning, for example, a Year 11 student asked me about all the required practicals. So, I made a six-page checklist. It wasn't particularly onerous to do but it covers every single required practical, every experiment and observation needed for your exams in science. I put it in my Google Classroom for my students and popped it in my "Buy Me a Coffee" shop for free, just as a little something for parents and students. It took me just five minutes this morning to do. I'm also branching out into doing remote courses because not everyone can afford tutoring. I'm putting together a science course for home-educated families that they can do remotely, just to make it a bit more affordable but also increase my passive income.

Two years ago, if you'd asked me where I wanted to be in five years' time, I would have said that I would have opened my own school and said to students: "I don't care what clothes you come in, so long as your clothing is appropriate." Everybody will be accepted, and we could have functional skills instead of maths and English, if that's what the students needed. We just would get stuff done, the right way. Two years ago, I'd have told you all about my ideas and plans for that. But now, I have a wonderful fiancé and my five-year plan is to be a stay-at-home mum. I'll earn a passive income from remote courses, maybe do a day of tutoring but nothing more, and I intend to live a slow and very meaningful life with my children, who probably will not go to school. If they want to go, I'll send them but if they decide it's not for them, I'll just withdraw them - no big deal. I've spent enough time living my life at a hundred miles an hour, chasing my tail. I've learnt my lesson. Now I would just like to live life slowly and enjoy my work-life balance with less money but more joy.

Vivienne's
KEY TAKEAWAYS

Many experts who had been in more senior roles chose to move away from leadership to gain a better work-life balance and improved working conditions. Despite the welcome opportunity to influence the culture, the extra responsibilities and levels of stress are perhaps not sufficiently well remunerated to make it worthwhile. For many teachers, it's the connections with their students that keeps them turning up to the job every day. With careful reflection and intentional action, we can purposely create daily opportunities to grow those connections, to increase their - and our - wellbeing. We also need to be intentional in planning future career development and skills acquisition in areas we find challenging– don't just leave that to the inset day and CPD sessions. Finding the right teaching route, whether that be in – or outside of - school is key to sustaining that passion for the craft that all good teachers have in common. And, as Jessica discovered, a move out of mainstream education might make you an even better teacher.

Reflection QUESTIONS

1. If you've been in a leadership role, what were the main rewards and challenges? How can you better support your colleagues?

_____

_____

_____

_____

2. How do you envisage your career developing in the next five years? What new roles or skills would you like to investigate to keep your career fulfilling?

_____

_____

_____

_____

3. Think of a meaningful interaction with a student. What did you learn, and how has it influenced your teaching approach?

_____

_____

_____

_____

4. Does traditional teaching still fit your needs? Would alternative roles like tutoring, consulting, or other paths align better with your goals?

_____

_____

_____

_____

CHAPTER FOUR
WHAT'S THE PROBLEM?

AP

I visit many schools and it's very unusual to meet somebody who hates the kids and the job; they might find the job really stressful, but almost everybody I speak to loves the work they do. They can appreciate how much they're appreciated. They know they make a difference. They know it's hard work, but nevertheless it's worthwhile work. That sense of purpose, that sense of doing something meaningful is very precious, but I think there are things that happen in schools that make you lose sight of it. If you are being told that you've got this mountain of marking that's got to be done in a particular way, then you haven't got time at the end of the day to go out and watch the kids in their football match. But if you did have time to go and see them, even if you were only there for 20 minutes and you saw that goal that Tom scored, it's worth so much. If you don't have the time at the end of the day to talk to your colleagues or make that phone call to a parent regarding a child that you're just worrying about a bit about, you diminish your place in that wider picture, beyond the instructional role in the classroom. There are lots of things that teachers are required to do that are, quite frankly, meaningless - and they know it. It just becomes exhausting.

We need to ensure we're giving teachers the tools they need to do their job and taking away the things that contribute very little. The lack of investment in the infrastructure for support services around schools needs to be turned around. We need support services. We need to have additional colleagues who can come in and advise us and support families. Because while teachers are expected to do all of that; trying to be a social worker alongside teaching is too hard. Teachers obviously care about their children and they're going to want to do that if there's no one else available. But that means it's too much. We need to really consider the tasks that we're asking teachers to do that are menial, admin type tasks. There's an opportunity with AI to engage much more in assessment that will be instantly available. There are some other really promising opportunities (not in AI, that doesn't mean you don't have to be the teacher anymore because you can just press a button on the machine and get on with it - not that kind of solution). At the heart of it, it's about being with children and enjoying children. It wouldn't take too much just to turn the dial a little and make things an awful lot better. Like reducing the accountability pressure, broadening definitions of children's success so it's not just all about the string of GCSEs, but a wide recognition that there are other forms of success that are very meaningful to children and make a difference.

Vivienne's **VIEWPOINT**

I asked Dame Alison about her involvement in the "Beyond Ofsted" report and whether their suggested changes would have a positive impact on issues around teacher recruitment and retention, particularly if schools could have access to a consultant adviser on a long-term basis.

AP

All our suggestions are just suggestions at present - we've got to see it come to fruition. It's very helpful that we've got a new Chief Inspector of Education who is bending over backwards to engage with the Chartered College and to engage with me. I've been asked to join an Ofsted teacher wellbeing reference group; even the fact that such a thing exists now is very encouraging. There's an offer to come and do a session with members and fellows where they can ask questions in an open environment. These are all things that the previous chief inspector wouldn't have dreamed of doing. It's all about culture. With a change of government, in my opinion, there will be a change to the way that Ofsted is organised. Under a different leadership there's a much more open approach to recognising that they don't always get everything right. There was a piece in The Guardian where Amanda Speilman (the previous chief inspector) defended Ofsted and said that they didn't do anything wrong in the Ruth Perry inspection. And I think, 'why are you still speaking up? You've had your day. Also: people don't agree with you - even the coroner didn't agree with you.'

Change is needed in terms of teacher recruitment and retention. It's complex. It's not just teaching that's suffering these issues; many professions are finding that post pandemic there's much less patience with the view that work should be your life. There's a much greater sense that life should be your life, and work is quite necessary around the edges. That's not something I've subscribed to (I've completely been a workaholic) but I can see that there is another way of doing things. I think it's partly that there should be greater flexibility in the way the school system works. Many youngsters actually thrived not being in school. Which says quite a lot about our school system, doesn't it? I completely get it. I mean, I didn't like going to school myself.

When I talked to the Conservative DFE consultation group about attendance during Covid, I said the last thing you want to be doing is fining families because there's been so much damage caused by the pandemic and people are feeling very fragile. The relationship between home and school has been fractured and we should be encouraging youngsters to come back, not forcing them. Of course, they didn't take any notice, being much more in favour of the sort of Jacob Rees-Mogg approach to bums on seats! I think there is a significant element of the teenage student population who would benefit from a combination of remote working and some socialisation in school, for those subjects that need a group – for example in most sports, arts and drama you need to be working collaboratively. But a lot of personal study can be done individually at home (if you've got space to do it - and not every child does). Just being away from the hurly burly can be helpful for many youngsters. There are things we do in the school system, that are necessary with a group of 30 that you wouldn't need to do if you were just working with an individual student or a small group (there's a whole array of things that are necessary in order to manage a building full of people). I just think it requires a bit more open-mindedness, although it's the kind of thing that politicians run a mile from, because for any party to say, "You don't need to come to school any more" would be political suicide! They are so terribly worried about standards and so on. When our eldest daughter, for example, got the syllabus for her A-levels she decided she was going to teach herself, although she was supposed to be in sixth form. She went to music because she loved it, but most of the time she studied at home and did exceptionally well.

LOD

What I disliked was the bureaucracy - the constant marking, admin, reporting that must be done. Also, the long hours and the burnout that accompanied that. There were ever-changing rules, priorities, scrapping the existing policy, introducing a new one; constant change and inconsistency in applying these policies - especially behaviour policies (SLT) or even finding anything that worked, really. By the time I'd finished my time as a teacher, behaviour at our school had reached an all-time low and there were genuine concerns for the reputation of the school in the community. With that, there was a real lack of respect from the middle leadership teaching roles. Typically, they had been there for a very long time, were far too comfortable in their positions and were seen as inefficient and lazy. So that combined to make me feel more demotivated, the longer I stayed on.

I think the number one issue teachers face is behaviour. There's nothing worse than feeling out of control in a classroom situation and if you're teaching a full five-hour day then that can be extremely exhausting, no matter how experienced you are. It doesn't matter if you're good or bad at behaviour management. If there are constant niggles, fights going on in the corridor and they are part of a whole-school behaviour problem it's a really tiring thing to deal with. You'd have some classes where there would be five or six 'characters' and the number would just be increasing every year, which clearly then affects the rest of the class, because it spoils the dynamic. One or two you can squash for behaviour but if there are quite a lot to deal with, it becomes an impossible task; you can't teach. You're there to teach, and they're not letting you.

We had that TikTok craze where kids were setting off fire alarms. There was a period of about six months where we had four or five fire alarms in a week and sometimes more than one in a day. Awful. The whole school was standing on the lawn in the rain. Then the saga of being sent the CCTV clips to try and identify the culprit. We made the punishment harsher and nipped it in the bud eventually. We were in the local papers again with another TikTok craze about writing in the toilets, because "it's a human right to be able to go to the toilet when you want to". Staff and student toilets were in a disgraceful state, because the kids would be hanging around in them and vandalising them during lesson times. They were literally ripping toilets out of the plumbing, cracking sinks, breaking locks and doors, graffitiing. There was a case of a staff iPad being stolen and an attempt to flush it down the toilet! SLT started getting staff to patrol the corridors and lock toilets, so they just did the same to staff and disabled toilets instead! Students across the country (including my school) started to riot. The kids had arranged it online – a whole school walkout. They refused to come back into lessons. We had kids throwing bins off roofs. One child escaped the school grounds and threw a brick through someone's window.

My school was well above average for children with EHCPs. There was considerable pressure to be an effective educator for these children that needed so much help and had such a complex background. I was a tutor, so I was involved in the pastoral side as well. One mother would literally call me every day. She didn't know what to do with her child or how to improve the situation and it was a nightmare for her.

Another big issue (more than pay) is general working conditions - how long your working day is and how much you're meant to be doing in those days, and how high stress all that work is. Although the recent strike action by teachers was in part triggered by insufficient pay, I wonder if it was more about the working conditions in the end. Personally, I felt that I'd prefer to have a better work life balance on the current pay scale, than to maintain or increase those levels of work on more pay.

There is a lack of career progression as well. The idea of me taking another chance on teaching and going through the interview process to go to another school to another head of department role just didn't seem worth it at the time. Because you have to make the decision on the day - you can't even discuss it with anyone first. And then what happens? Where do you go from there? You want even more responsibility, which comes with more stress and less job satisfaction. And it's a pyramid: the higher up you go, the less available roles there are.

I always say that teachers do two jobs. They have the actual teaching element, which in itself could be a full timetable day and the other is an office job where you deal with paperwork, complaints and meetings all the time. I was very often doing 12-hour days, and occasionally I'd have to stay longer - especially if it was a parents' evening that finished at 9.30pm or something ridiculous like that – or an open evening or theatre trip. The only proper holiday was a summer holiday, because the week-long half terms plus at least a week of Christmas and Easter holidays were all report writing, planning and marking. As soon as the holidays hit, I got ill, and I thought, What, again? What is the point in this? I can't even enjoy my time off!

KP

Currently there are a number of issues, including teachers being overworked and not having any recognition. The media have demonised teachers as people that have 13 weeks off a year, but they've no clue how it works. Behaviour in schools is a massive issue. We've seen it all over the news, haven't we? There have been articles out about teachers finally admitting that behaviour in the classroom is appalling and attributing it to mobile phones, sexism… I also think

49

micromanagement is a problem. Lots of academies don't give teachers autonomy over what or how to get through the curriculum. Accountability for me was one of the biggest things. Young people who needed to be in a classroom often weren't having their needs met and didn't really care about being there. You'd phone up parents and wonder how to make a difference without their support in wanting their children to be successful at education.

If you're in a toxic environment, and that's not going to change, it is hard. Whether that's because of leadership or student behaviour, if you're not supported by the other adults within the establishment that you work in then it's impossible to find a happy place and to feel as though you're making a difference or being successful. Teachers put themselves on the line all the time and if things aren't going well, it could feel like an attack on you as a person rather than the anonymity of sitting at a desk in an office job and receiving a horrible email. As a teacher you're constantly evaluating what you've done. You're more likely to focus on the things that didn't go well than celebrate the things that did. It's very rare for parents to phone up school and say, "Your teachers are amazing!" and if it does happen the head usually gives a huge assembly about it!

SG

Fashions in teaching come and go. But after teaching for a long time, you realise it's always the same - they're trying to reinvent the wheel. Basically, the students are just kids and that is often forgotten. How can you find a way to reach these kids, to make them learn something? Socrates, who is the father of education, says you must do it yourself in order to learn. We are losing that in England; we are spoon feeding students the information, rather than, "This is how you do it. Now you do it." Because when they do it themselves the responsibility is back on them. They are more likely to learn, because they're putting your teaching into practice. We must be accountable for the students. Teachers are focusing too much on providing everything they can, in order to demonstrate they have supplied all the resources, to show that they have done their job properly. Unfortunately, teachers always have to justify, to make sure they cover their backs and give sufficient evidence when they have an appraisal. Parents also can be quick to blame us for not providing their children with all the information, so we need to provide evidence for them too. This culture is damaging because it doesn't allow teachers to relax and be themselves, to be all they can – or push pupils to be independent enough. In my subject you also cannot always be the entertainer. Grammar lessons can be dry, but they are necessary, especially in Key Stage Four. You try to make lessons engaging but sometimes students just have to be resilient and focus, listen to the explanation.

Nowadays we are driven by stats and numbers. For example, my Year 9 French class has been working so hard, considering the fact that a few months ago they were just Year 8. They have just turned 13 and they're at the mercy of their hormones. It's completely new work for them and they are working so hard in French and I'm very pleased. They had their assessment recently, and most of them got 78% to 95%! However, we were asked to break them down into the top 20%, then the middle and the lower bands. The school decided that: for the upper band to have "sufficient progress" on their report, they must have 90%

in their assessment! It's so unrealistic! Some students had 85% and they will be given a "not making progress" for that! For a start, nobody told them they were in the upper band, so I did. I said, "Whatever your tracking shows, I want you to be aware that as your teacher I know that you work super hard and I'm actually very pleased with your work and your progress. I'm following the rules here, but your tracking won't show what I really think of you." Because that can really crush someone's confidence. This way of putting them in a box with numbers, it's completely wrong. Currently, I think there must be a risk of some schools artificially raising or lowering actual figures in order to show the right progress.

Without sounding too pro-French, I have noticed that English literacy levels in our kids have dropped. If students knew more advanced vocabulary in English, they wouldn't have a problem in French. After all, it is true that 45% of the English language is based on French. That is very difficult for students with a very low level of literacy but if they read more and knew this advanced vocabulary, French would be so much easier for them. They also struggle with learning English grammar rules and this creates problems in French as well.

Avoiding overload is about sticking to exactly what you need so no one gets lost or goes off at a tangent or creates extra work for themselves. Most of the teachers I've met are very creative and they could easily create wonderful projects that would probably be fun to do, but we don't have time, unfortunately. These days parents expect good exam results. The students need to get the grades if they want to do further education, so these creative projects just become a luxury we can't afford. If we had the time, if we didn't do duty during break or lunch time, after school, before school, if we didn't have the meeting after school or before school, if we didn't have parents evening, if we didn't have the interventions with the kids, if we didn't have to write thousands of emails, if we didn't have marking; I would love to organise a foreign exchange or festival and it would be fantastic but…

I would love to actually work for a school which is confident enough to say, "We don't need the data because we are focusing so much on making sure that teachers have time to teach these kids the best possible thing that they are going to follow and we're going to inspire them and they're going to be lifelong learners".

The trouble is, that's quite risky, because if you then want to go to university and you don't have the grades, then you might not get in. So, we are stuck with the current system and maybe it then falls to the parents to provide that extra bit of cultural education. However, there are so many children in circumstances where that's not always possible and we have to be aware of that.

Teachers put up with a lot; the main thing is that we are up against a system that doesn't recognise our work. There's a lack of recognition amongst peers. I don't understand this sense of competition – if I see a teacher that gets good results, it spurs me on, it inspires me to be a better teacher myself. It doesn't make me feel jealous or resentful!

When you're starting in the profession, those kinds of things will happen; it will be hard. They're not always going to help and you may not know if you're doing the right thing. You're going to feel like you're drowning. You have to be humble and accept that you're learning, that you won't get it right straight away. You also need to have the courage to ask others to help you because you are a learner and you have never been put in this position before.

I always try to help colleagues if I can because I know how it feels. When we see a teacher that's struggling, I think it's our duty to stop and say, "OK, let's have a chat." The other day in the staff room there was a science teacher swearing in frustration at his computer. I heard him, but he didn't realise I'd heard him. I was about to go home but instead I sat down next to him and said, "How are you feeling?" I barely speak to him normally, but because that happened, he started to confide in me and tell me all these things. You could tell it helped him to not feel alone. I can't even remember exactly what we discussed - and it doesn't matter. The idea is just that he had somebody who listened to him at exactly the right moment. I heard him, I could relate to what he said, and we were sharing experiences.

Vivienne's **VIEWPOINT**

I thanked SG for saying that because that is one of the major reasons for writing this book and working with teachers in a coaching capacity. I want people to feel they're not alone. Everybody does need to be able to tell their story and be able to just vent about their day when times are tough. If teachers could do that with someone who acts as a neutral, yet concerned sounding board more often, they would probably have the longevity that they would like, because they don't have to bottle it all up and try to suppress it.

GP

The main issues faced by teachers today are firstly that underfunding of resources and support staff has meant there is too much pressure to fulfil so many parts of teaching and learning in a classroom. The SEND funding in particular and reduction in support staff - due to poor salaries and training - has really affected teachers.

Secondly, I think that behaviour and technology have a huge impact, including poor support from parents. When teachers work so hard to plan and prepare resources and progression for their lessons, sometimes it can be undermined by poor behaviour, abuse of mobile phones and a poor attitude that has been encouraged by poor parenting. Quite often parents who have struggled in school or resent education themselves have also passed these feelings (even unconsciously) down to their children.

As for what I personally dislike about teaching: maybe I'm weathered in my years, but my biggest struggle is pedagogical structure that is forced down from above (whether governmental or internal). I feel I've tried and tested so many, I've found what works and sometimes struggle with having to force a square peg into a round hole to tick a box.

SEC

Why are so many people leaving teaching? I don't think it's the money. There is a lack of recognition in society... I also think there must be a calculation that people make in their heads about this level of constant stress which is applied because of the exam machine. You have to make these grades. Your students have to perform like this (irrespective of all the reasons why we know each individual student doesn't). If we have time to do that, there's got to be a calculation that teachers are making, particularly the younger ones, about whether they're earning enough money in order to justify this.

I think that what has changed to a certain extent is a byproduct of the politics and it's also evident in the NHS. A lot of the conditions that used to exist that you put up with are now seriously medicalised and people want attention because of that medicalised imagery and that expectation. It's happened in education as well. When looking at our success and results, considering our base for English it became reasonable, when our partners were looking at what we were doing, that they were saying there is not a quality assurance experience across all classes. I think we had to conform to that because it's a reasonable request. But in doing so, we went to everybody teaching the same thing roughly at the same time. Fortunately, in our school there was still a level of autonomy within that. All the teachers bought into it because it did make it easier for students to move across groups if there were behavioural issues or friendship problems. It did level out the experience because everybody was getting the same input. I'm talking about the comprehensive system. I don't know how it works in the private system. It is a reasonable requirement, but what it's done is suck the joy out of what we were able to freely do. Some schools have become exam factories because they're just focusing exactly on the skills bases needed to pass the exams and where before there'd be days where children could harangue Shakespeare insults across the room, or you could take them to the hall and get them to run Romeo and Juliet through with paper swords: all of that has gone. There's no time. It has to be measurable. There have to be assessments. The students have lost a lot of the joy, and our figures speak for themselves. We don't get the number of A-level students we used to, because it's not so much fun as it used to be.

All teachers still feel that they want to raise lifelong readers and encourage a love of literature. To achieve that as well, you're either going to have to do that extracurricular or mechanise certain aspects, like enforcing a period of silent reading at the start of every lesson. But it is just this exam pressure and the lack of flexibility.

We have talked as a department and with other professionals repeatedly about what was it, when was it that it changed and why and how and nobody can actually pinpoint that change of mindset in our students. There are so many things to factor into it. There's a psychologist called Jonathan Haidt who's just written a book called "The Anxious Generation: How the Great Rewiring of Childhood is Causing an Epidemic of Mental Illness." They've stemmed the anxiety of teenage children to the date when smartphones came in (not so much mobiles, but smartphones) so that they were able to withdraw from their societal groups and they weren't studying with each other anymore.

There's also a spoon-feeding issue where students are now expecting that slideshow format. They don't have to do independent research, they are just given whatever they need. The knock-on effect of that (and it's been really obvious in the last couple of years), is that students are worse. It's the opposite of what we hoped was going to happen. They are unable to apply what they know to what they see because they're not used to having to do any of the thinking for themselves.

All the pedagogy and all the ideas about independent learning or whatever the current name for any of this is - it's not working because students don't have the general knowledge that they used to have. They don't have knowledge about how to research. They also don't have the computer literacy that you think they would have - it's limited to their requirements for their functional social life. This doesn't apply to all students but it's almost like learned helplessness, where students stare at you. They say, "I don't get this. Give me a sentence starter. Give me a grid. Give me a template and then I can think." What's changed in the last year in teaching as part of the CPD at my school is that they've been asking us to look at things in order to make changes, and one of them is making sure that students can think for themselves. So, I am now no longer just giving the answer. I'm doing much more scaffolding of how to think - not how to apply whatever it is you know, but how to think around how you're doing it. The questions might be, "Here is this case study. You tell me how you're going to approach it," instead of, "let's highlight the keywords - here they are." I didn't train to teach like that. That's the thing that worries me most: the inability to think because if these students can't think, how are they going to go to university? And are the universities doing the same thing as us, effectively?

When it comes to subject knowledge I am quite concerned, in English, about how little some of our student teachers have actually read - some have virtually no knowledge of anything before the beginning of the 20th Century and a lack of wider cultural awareness, due to insufficient wider reading.

When students get to A-level, I think that it is getting better but sometimes the students are very non-verbal. They don't want to contribute verbally anymore but then they produce work that shows that they have taken in a lot of what you said and it's surprising. So there's this mismatch between their ability or confidence to communicate verbally and what they can produce on paper.

Vivienne's VIEWPOINT

The Department of Education's decision to take the spoken component out of the marked section of GCSE English Language exam was, I believe, regrettable and has resulted in oracy being perceived as a lesser value skill, whereas the Sutton Trust found that 97% of teachers saw life skills – including oracy – as equally important to academic qualifications (if not more so). Thankfully, the tide seems to be turning towards providing opportunities to learn **to** talk as well as **through** talk, although the biggest barriers to a whole-school oracy approach in state schools are not enough teaching time (48%), not enough staff time (46%) and not enough teacher training and development (46%). The teachers I work with in CPD sessions all recognise the value of oracy and are finding creative ways to include it in every subject.

SEC

There is a significantly larger number of students that I'm taking in at A-level who have literacy challenges (often undiagnosed), which makes it less accessible for them in terms of the higher level teaching that we were used to providing.

Teachers who trained during the pandemic came into the profession at the worst possible time. I don't know whether we considered enough what the impact was on the teachers, not just the students. Also, I think if you were disenfranchised, disenchanted with teaching before the pandemic, it would have confirmed your feeling because you had different stresses, but you were able to reflect whether this was actually a job that was worth the mental health demands that it made - and the long hours. That changed things for me: I stopped working quite so many hours afterwards; I decided I wasn't going to go on doing 12 to 14 hour days and then go home and continue thinking about work.

I felt particularly sorry for those teachers who were also parents and who were having to manage both sides of the equation. I think that must have exhausted them. Many of us found we were teaching into thin air. There were four or five kids (if you had a top set) that were actually present but the rest of them were just folding up their computers and putting them under their pillows.

Fundamentally students may have felt they didn't need to be at school ever again, because they could do what they needed (well, those that had got sufficient GCSE maths skills). Because of their ability to contact each other on social media, I don't think the social issues were as serious as they might have been had we been in the 1917 flu epidemic, where no one saw anybody at all. So they lost the feeling that school was listening and their confidence in the concept of school. They also missed a lot of work and became less able to work independently and self-start.

My 16-year-old student hadn't handed in her coursework, and when I asked why she hadn't done it, she said, "Because I don't want to." For the first time ever, I thought, "I have no come back to this." However, her favourite subject was art; I went through this poetry collection and found one that was so obviously visual and colour driven, and I read it out loud to her as performance poetry. Once she started talking about how it operated, then she was happy to start writing. I think they do need to talk about it first. Often, it's "I don't know how to do this. I don't know how to think about all of this intellectually. I don't know how to think about what you're asking me to do, so therefore I don't want to do it because it's too much of a risk." A lot of the time it's, "I don't want to fail. But I'm with other people who seem to be able to do this. People might be judging me…" We've lost the time and capacity to interrogate the individual skills of the students.

Interestingly, in health and social care, it's different from English because you are teaching very personal or difficult areas so you do need a little bit of interrogation and understanding of the students' backgrounds, or it can be a minefield. For instance, we have students that have siblings with conditions that we study. We have students who've come from abusive homes and we rely very much on the pastoral team to advise us. But it has taken us quite a long time to explain to them that this is a need-to-know basis from a safeguarding point of view. If you do have time, particularly with those students with special educational needs, to establish where their schematic backgrounds lie, then you stand a chance.

Society and the press constantly remind us of our marvellous long holidays, but until parents and politicians come in and see what we actually do, they don't understand that if we didn't have those holidays, we'd all be broken within two years. The holidays arrive just at the point where people are on the verge of a nervous breakdown and then you spend half the holiday just recovering - or being ill, because that's the only time you can be ill!

Some of the new or young teachers still maintain incredible professionalism but - certainly where I work - their timetables are so heavy, their classes are so large, and the extreme ends of the behaviour disrupt the purpose of the room so significantly they feel they're actually failing when they're not. If you're being dropped in on and being critiqued as well: that all adds to the sense of failure.

The full formal model of observation, where they would be in maybe for the whole lesson was traumatic for the teacher. But the drop-ins I think are almost as traumatic because they're not long enough and you can't explain to the drop-in, "This is what we're doing and we've just done that, but we're working towards that."

We don't seem to have quite got the coaching mechanism right, so that those teachers who are being looked at don't feel it's punitive or fear they might be moving on to some sort of support plan where everything is being done that should be done, but it still doesn't feel that it's genuine.

What teachers need sometimes is: "OK, you need to come out of the classroom for 25 minutes - go and sit down", or: "OK, this isn't working. That child needs to move", which isn't viable. People are kind. They try to support, but if you're burning your teachers out repeatedly, or you're giving them classes that they can't manage early in their career, you're just going to put them off. You're going to make the fields of their failures when they're not, when even senior teachers can't manage those classes. But then you don't want to give only your senior teachers the difficult classes, because then they're destroyed by it.

JM

The teaching world's quite brutal, isn't it? I wrote my car off on the M62 one morning. When you write your car off on a motorway, the police, the highway agency, the highway patrol maintenance all arrive and I got an ambulance sent to me as well, because my airbags deployed. When the impact happened, I slid forwards in my seat, and I smashed my knees against the driving column, under the steering wheel and fractured my kneecap. I didn't know that at the time, because obviously adrenaline blocks that pain you're in. In the back of the ambulance, they told me, "You can't go to work. We need to take you to the hospital!"

I said, "Yeah, I'm totally fine. I need to go to work! I'm a teacher." It was the second to last day of school before Christmas and I was supposed to be giving my test results back to the students before they broke up. I felt such an obligation to get my backside to work that I made my mother pick me up from the hard shoulder on the motorway, and then drive me the rest of the way. When I arrived, they let me teach until the adrenaline wore off, and I started violently vomiting and shaking. Then they had to call me an ambulance, and I went to hospital and found out that I had broken my kneecap and had a severe concussion!

My grandad had been in hospital and died suddenly in the middle of the night. I hadn't been to visit because I had to work the next day. Even after my auntie told me the news: the next day I woke up, got ready, and went to work. I didn't want to set cover - setting cover is just as hard as doing the actual day's work. My best friend popped into the classroom, to say good morning and asked if I was alright. Then it really hit me that he was gone, and I completely broke down and was absolutely sobbing. I had one of those classrooms where half the wall was made of glass, so we huddled under my desk, to hide me. A member of leadership came to see me and said, "The kids are coming up in five minutes; pull yourself together." Right at the end of the day, that same member of staff came back and admitted, "I'm really sorry - I probably should have sent you home". By then I'd had to switch off, to turn off my emotions and numb myself out to get through the day.

I used to put on this bright, cheery, smiling face. It's what comes naturally to me now, but I used to put it on. But then my face just dropped, and I once got caught by a member of staff, and they said

"Jesus Christ, I saw that switch there!"

And I said, "I'm so exhausted, that's all. It's just fake. You just turn it on, and then you're done, and it just disappears, you know?"

It's bizarre having to perform like that. There's no escape from it, either. I once got pulled aside and told, "You need to cheer up in the staff room a bit, because you're bringing the mood down!"

I was thinking, "I'm so sorry that my emotional exhaustion from teaching all day is starting to impact all the people. But how do you think I feel?"

Then it was: "Why aren't you integrating with the team? You're not being much of a team player, are you?"

"Well, you literally just told me last week that I'm bringing the mood down. So I pulled myself away because I'm trying to do what you want me to do" …

But they said, "You need to eat lunch with everyone. You can't eat lunch in your classroom, but you just need to cheer up a bit!"

We work endlessly. It spills into weekends. You spend your Saturday just trying to recover from the week, and Sunday prepping for the next. It's a cycle. You're just trying to catch a breath, and there's always more to do. It's truly maddening.

You've got two days at the weekend, but because you've been so exhausted you've not kept the house tidy during the week. I used to say Saturday was my day for lounging about and recovering, or maybe trying to do something fun. On Sunday I would be cleaning the house and prepping meals to take to work and meals for the evening, so that if there was a day where I was particularly drained and I couldn't think of something to cook, it was there for me.

I picked the wrong subject in terms of marking, because in science they do six exams. When mock exams season comes round the Key Stage Three kids aren't bad. They usually only do two papers. But by the time you get to Year 10 you have three papers per child and in Year 11, you have six papers and if you have two Year 11 classes and you've got 30 kids in each class... Foundation isn't too bad, because there's more ticking of boxes, so you could fly through a bit quicker. But when you get onto higher and you've got five-mark multi-step equations and six-mark evaluations, you've got to really sit there and read it and think. But what you're actually thinking to yourself is: if I don't get all this done now, I'm going to have to spend the entire week next week, and if I can't get this done by this day, I'm not going to be able to go out with my family. Because hell hath no fury if you don't do that data entry by 3 o'clock on the Friday - during the holidays. They deliberately put the mocks before the holidays, so that the teachers have time to mark them. I've cancelled family days out. I've taken marking on holiday with me before. It's absolutely ridiculous.

SMA

I had worked as an IT engineer in several schools where I had the opportunity to meet and talk to young people. I also met plenty of teachers. I felt like they were doing what was right for young people and they never seemed that stressed. Having gone into teaching myself, however, it's completely different from what I thought it was on the outside.

At the school I'm in I feel like 30% is the teaching and 70%, is everything else that goes with it. Many students are not really taking responsibility for their learning and teachers are doing more work than they should. Coming from a culture where education is not always free, so it's regarded as a gift and teachers are highly esteemed because they're there to impart knowledge, it's kind of a shock to me.

A lot of the time I'm awake in the night thinking, "OK, what am I going to do with this class?" Because each class is different – even though it's the same subject, the student dynamics are so different, and you need to find a strategy that works with each of those students before you teach. I imagined it would all be smooth sailing: go into class to deliver your lesson, the students take responsibility for their learning, you give them great support, you mentor them and give them every resource they need to pass…

I feel that we spend so much time thinking about the students' mental health, but not enough thinking about the teachers' mental health.

Vivienne's VIEWPOINT

I feel like part of the struggle teachers face is thinking that everyone else is managing apart from them. I remember my NQT year, where I was made a co-tutor. There was a big mental health awareness drive going on in the school, so the tutor time focus was invariably on how to improve mental wellbeing and promote confidence and resilience. The students would roll their eyes and moan, "Oh no – not this again!" I, on the other hand sat there thinking wryly to myself how ironic it was that pretty much all the symptoms the PowerPoint described related to me and how close to the edge I felt on a daily basis, yet it felt like nobody had really noticed and this was neither the time nor place to reveal my real state of mind.

SMA

One of the things I'm seriously struggling with is that the teaching's almost at the mercy of that kid that is not working. You have to find a way to engage them, give them a task, come back in five minutes to help, but then it's not finished, so you say "Have another try" and you give them another 10 minutes. But there are four of them, so you keep checking if they've done the task or not but it's a class of 30 – one of them is going to end up by going home and complaining that the teacher didn't give them enough support! You have 30 in a class, just you on your own. Every child should get the best of you. Every child should get the same level of experience of support in the classroom. We've got different abilities. I get it. That's when the extra support will come in but sometimes it's just not logistically possible. We give them detentions for lack of work, to come back and complete it in that time. I asked one parent to make sure their son attended, but they weren't that bothered, as he was on track for a grade four. I explained that he was not doing sufficient coursework to be awarded one. Their response was to ask if there was a model of what we were doing for him to look at instead...

I'm finding that some parents feel that if their child doesn't pass it's the teacher's fault and sometimes I feel I get blamed for that child not doing any work. If you don't like the teacher, is that an excuse for you not to do well in your studies? Also, if the student has not worked in their double lesson with you and then you give up your time after school (which you really need for doing other work like planning) for a catch-up session, which they don't attend and then they don't achieve the expected grades, who's at fault?

There are people that I have spoken to, of diverse cultures, who grew up in this country but who are older and things that they've mentioned really resonate with me. They worry about the next generation because they feel like they lack respect and that technology is taking over, that they spend more time on TikTok and Instagram than doing their homework. Now, I'm not against technology – how could I be, in my subject? - but I can see their point. My students often tell me that homework should be banned, that schoolwork should stay at school and home is for relaxing and doing other things, so there are two arguments.

One thing I've always understood is that whatever you learn in school, you come back home to revise. That is the only way you can retain the knowledge. I always say to students that whatever you are taught in school, remember there are 30 of you in the class, so you need to strengthen your knowledge by looking at it afterwards and say, "OK, what did we look at today?" That's what we used to do. For example, they taught us fractions in class but to make sure I really got it, I'd go home and just practise myself. We don't have that now. No, they'd rather go on their Xbox to play games for hours, up to even four o'clock in the morning. Now, when they come to school, they say, "Oh Miss, I'm tired!"

I spend far too much time worrying about finding the right approach to help my students – and when I'm not doing that, I am marking or planning lessons. I don't have enough time for myself. I don't have enough time to spend with my family. There are 13 us in my wider family and that doesn't include any school age children. I'm the only one who teaches, and the others don't always want to go on holiday at the most expensive times of the year!

When I talk about discipline, I'm going to refer to the background I come from and also the fact that in my family, discipline is a priority for us. Unfortunately, the students that take most of our time, the ones we spend the most effort on, are the ones who expect to do whatever they like. You could have 30 students in a class and 25 of them are ready to learn, but if five of them are saying, "it's not for me" and wasting everybody's time it will negatively affect the 25 others and probably even impact their grades. If discipline is not being enforced and one kid gets away with something, then others will follow suit and you begin to see a pattern of that behaviour.

It depends on the environment and the area and the attitude of the parents. In the two state schools in London (where I trained) I never saw the kind of behaviour or the attitude of entitlement that I'm seeing in my current school. Sometimes in lessons children will act as if they're doing you a favour! Maybe as this is a more affluent area it's different because some children seem a bit arrogant? But in the other schools I mentioned, the parents there had the position that education is a priority, so we'll support you, but the learning is your responsibility. Own your education. When I talk to my friends who are teachers in London and share some of my experiences in this school, they just look at me in disbelief!

I've talked to a lot of teachers and even the ones who have 20 years' experience are finding behaviour worrying. If there's a shortage of teachers, why are there people starting their careers and quitting in the second year? It's a rewarding job but a lot of teachers are retraining and leaving teaching altogether. A lot of the time it's because of behaviour.

I'm open to sharing a couple of incidents with you because I want people to know that these things happened and to learn from it. These are stories that I have told my friends and family.

I think it was the first year that I started teaching. I'm kind of relaxed with my classes. I want them to feel they can approach me, discuss things with me and have a laugh. A lot of students go home and tell their parents that I'm "chilled". One day a kid came into class with a piece of paper and said, "Oh Miss, my friend said to show you this".

And out of interest, I took the paper.

When I opened it up there was this picture of an ape printed on coloured paper. You know, a monkey thinking.

As a person of colour, I'm not one that usually reacts when it comes to like a racial abuse or anything; you know, it's empowerment - I embrace it and I overlook things. For some reason though, this touched me and I almost broke down in tears. I'd just heard on the news that Marcus Rashford, the Manchester United player, had recently been racially abused and for me to be shown that when I got to school the same day, come on! This happened to be a child that I'd been giving extra support to in the class. I just walked out of the room.

I gave the picture to my supervisor and said, "Look what happened." They put the child in detention. That was all. Then an email came from the parent saying that I went too far. Why did I have to put her child in detention? Because they think that I'm a cool teacher and because I'm cool, they can say things like that to me. She said I'd taken it out of context, that I shouldn't have reacted the way I did. I just didn't reply. I don't think anybody else did, or whether it was reported.

I was really disturbed. If I, as a teacher, felt like that, what about other students who are in the school? What else do they get to see that they can't tell their parents? What are they dealing with every single day that we don't get to see? The way I reacted was not just about myself but also the other people in the school of the same colour as me.

The second experience was when a child (that wasn't doing so well in lessons and was very destructive) brought a water toy into class. I teach in the computer lab and of course water and electricity don't mix! Somehow, I managed to get that water pistol away from him and I put it right at the top of my classroom cupboard. Before I knew it, he got out of his seat at the back. I knew what he was heading for, so I ran straight to where my desk was because I didn't want him to take it and risk him spraying water all over the computers. Then I logged it as a detention and that was the end of it (or so I thought).

The next thing was that I got an email from his mother claiming that I'd pushed him into a cupboard! By the way, this is the same child who had previously stolen my clicker (twice!) and his mum had to replace it. They logged it as a formal complaint, so the school had to investigate. They interviewed all the students in the classroom, including the ones that were not in that day! The students confirmed how helpful I'd always been, that "Miss was only trying to help us pass because we didn't have a Year 9 IT teacher" and it's true - since I've had them from Year 10 my focus has simply been to support them to pass, which confirmed that this wouldn't have been in character for me. That these other pupils stepped forward said a lot, I think. After they'd done the investigations and meetings, I was free to go but the student and I had to have a restorative justice meeting. I might have felt tearful, but I stayed as solid as a rock. The school said that at least we only had a few more months together and they promised to give me some extra support when that student was in lessons, because there were other tricky students as well. In the end I had just one lesson of support and that was the end of it.

EP

I think one of the reasons why so many teachers leave in the UK is not actually work-life balance, because for most of us, teaching is an important part of our lives. It's finding space for you to exist as a self within all of that and balancing your needs with the needs of your workplace.

It comes back to being asked to somehow depart from who you are in order to fulfil someone's unrealistic expectations of what's possible. It can take a bit of trial and error to find yourself a school that has the work culture, ethos and levels of empathy needed to thrive as an individual, because you don't know what you're looking for at the beginning. When you're on your interview day and you're being shown around a school it's very different. They're trying to present their best face to encourage you to work there. If they offer you the role, you're expected to accept then and there, without any time to reflect on it all or compare it to somewhere else (because you might have found somewhere even better). People working in corporate jobs might interview across a two-week period. If somebody offers them a contract or sends them a job offer, they can say, "Thank you. I have two more interviews this week. I'll get back to you next week and let you know." They're in a position to ask, "How negotiable is the salary or the flexible working directives?" Whereas (even if you've got an interview the next day) in teaching, it's very much at the discretion of the headteacher to allow you to respond after you've had that interview.

Vivienne's **VIEWPOINT**

One school I applied for took two weeks to decide whether they were going to take me on for a one-year contract, whereas I had to show interest straight away. I remember my university tutor being furious on my behalf and saying this was highly irregular, but I really wanted to work there…

EP

Teaching salaries are not competitive when compared to other roles that require a postgraduate qualification. Out of teachers I've trained up, there are a lot of people who are coming into teaching or who are already in teaching, but don't possess the requisite degree in a related area or subject knowledge to be teaching that at secondary level. Teacher training isn't always fit for purpose in terms of adequately preparing people for the workplace – or failing people who shouldn't be teachers. Universities need the funding and they're incentivised not to fail people.

What I **don't** love about teaching is that the lack is a constant. To quote J. R. R. Tolkien and Bilbo Baggins, "I feel thin, sort of stretched, like butter scraped over too much bread." It's being spread very thinly. It's not being able to do things because you haven't got the time or energy. You haven't got the budget. You haven't got the SLT permission to do an out of school trip. Some colleagues will try and squeeze themselves ever smaller so they can just fit in an extra bit. They're the ones who are waking up at four o'clock in the morning so they can get some work done before they get to work. They are physically falling apart with hip problems and back problems and chronic flare-ups of psoriasis (not to mention the mental toll), who are martyring themselves for the job. It's constantly snipping off bits of yourself, whether it's your personal life, whether it's the time that you'd be spending on yourself doing other things, or spending your own money buying supplies or paying for subscriptions to enhance your work. It's, "I'll just do a little bit more," until you realise that you've worn everything smooth and there isn't anything to hold on to properly.

There's a past paper on homelessness and poverty with an extract from a Caitlin Moran article about being poor, that there's a heaviness to poverty. She talks about how everything gets you down when you're poor, so you need things to pep you up: a sugary treat, a cigarette, something just to lift you a little bit. That resonated with me because this is like teaching! A lot of us are struggling. A lot of teachers use food banks or struggle to pay their bills. But even without that, the poverty of experience, the poverty of time, the poverty of energy and empathy…teachers are drinking or smoking too much or eating too much sugar because we need little lifts - temporary as they may be - to pull us out of the doom and gloom.

I went to a teaching event at a posh private school recently. They had better facilities and a larger number of extracurriculars they could offer because they have the time and budget. They have double the teaching staff to student ratio we do. It's not just about class size - the teachers are not teaching as many hours per week. In the UK state sector, we teach more contact hours in the classroom than almost anyone else on the continent and almost anyone else in EEC countries. Other places prioritise things like planning and preparation. The maximum number of teaching contact hours allowed in the French state sector is 18. The rest of your week is made up of time where you can plan, prepare, mark and even collaborate with your colleagues, whereas we're made to do that after school hours, or on our weekends. In the private sector they teach less contact hours than we do but they still teach more than schools in other countries. Schools don't employ enough staff to make sure that they have the time during the week to do their jobs.

Everyone in teaching works some weekends. When you're training everything is too much. You are getting your head around things. You haven't learnt how to be efficient yet or how to prioritise things and you're always being asked to do more than is feasible. I remember being advised to try to make sure that at least one day on your weekend is a day off. I don't think I ever actually got there during my training year. I think I managed it in my first year of teaching (sort of). But the idea is that on the two days a week when you're not being paid, you're still supposed to spend one whole day working. Most teachers spend half a day to a day at weekends - even the ones who are very experienced, who have a bank of resources, who know what they're doing. If you're diligent and you want to keep on top of things, support students and not just become a content delivery machine you **have to**, because there isn't any other time during the week.

Good private sector schools now mostly require a teacher training qualification but there is no legal requirement to be a qualified teacher to work there, so there's a huge variation in quality and value for parents' money. In the one I visited, though, I was struck by the calm self-confidence of both students and staff. There were a lot of students from wealthy backgrounds but quite a few were there on bursaries and scholarships. I noticed the lack of feeling rushed or squeezing things in, partly because in a boarding school you have the luxury of more time as children don't go home at the end of the day.

You'll know as well as I do the horror of cover...I don't think there's been a single week this academic year where my school hasn't put on a day of 'supervised study': a hundred students in the school hall with two or three adults, doing silent work on their own and not actually getting specialist teaching at all because the cover demand has been too high. The problem is partly that we're all exhausted. We're all being burnt at both ends and we don't take days off until it's impossible to continue and you have to take two or three days off in a row. Even if your empathetic colleagues ask, "Should you be in today? You don't look well at all," there isn't any top-down policy in place to advise not to come in if you are unwell - the margins are too tight. The most your head of department might say is, "You really ought to go home before period six." They won't say, "Good God! You look terrible! Go home now and don't come in for the rest of the week!" because the sheer increase in workload for everyone would cause logistical nightmares. You hear uncharitable comments (born from frustration rather than ill-will) about people on long-term sick leave and nobody wants to fail their colleagues, so there is shame associated with needing to take time off. Consequently, the next time you're sick you think, "What are they going to be saying about me?"

Empathy fatigue — as a self-preservation measure - is a real thing if you're constantly surrounded by suffering. You see it with the children: ever since Covid we've had serious problems across the country with persistent absence from students, particularly those with anxiety. And parents are keeping their kids off when they're sick more when they used to just send them in. There isn't the time, space or emotional capacity to take this opportunity to overhaul the way we operate in schools and the expectations we have. You might have a severely anorexic kid who can't be in school, whose parents are getting letters home telling them they're going to be fined for persistent absence. At parents evening you're told to explain that they're not going to do as well as predicted. Yet their child is possibly dying - maybe that should be the priority here instead! Increasingly there's this obsession with attendance figures and how they affect attainment.

Vivienne's **VIEWPOINT**

Of course, with first-hand experience of teaching in one, I would say that maybe these children need to be spending some time in an alternative provision centre, so that they can continue to maintain that link with education but be in a place where they can actually do some work whilst feeling safe, comfortable and not too stressed.

EP

Parents come to us saying they think their child may be autistic and ask us to diagnose them. But we have to tell them to go through their GP, which will probably be about a five-year wait, by which time the child will have outgrown the child and adolescent mental health system and therefore they'll have to wait another five years in the adult system. And it's not just painful knowing there are things you want to do to help (which I'm sure is the case in a lot of the caring professions that have had their budget slashed). It's knowing that you can't even signpost to other services.

A lot of kids who are neurodivergent in some way can mask well enough to appear to be doing fine when actually, if they were given access arrangements that allowed them to work at the same amount of effort as their peers, they would be flying. They're having to work twice as hard to get to where their less capable peers are.

I know where the levers are within the school system, so I know where to tell others to push. I've done that and I stand by it but at the same time there is a sense of disloyalty to the institution. Thankfully I think I'm just a bit of a nuisance, rather than 'the enemy'. I think my frame of mind is very much that I work for the kids, not for the school. So that is the way I come at it. And I choose my battles because if I went in swinging all the time, I wouldn't have any breath left in my body!

Vivienne's
KEY TAKEAWAYS

Teachers enjoy the core aspects of the job (such as forming connections and making a meaningful contribution), but this can be overshadowed by admin overload and meaningless tasks. Schools would benefit from better investment into support systems and additional staff members. Poor leadership, poor student behaviour and inconsistent policies, compounded by a lack of support from SLT and parents, lead to disillusionment and demotivation. To reduce teacher attrition rates and support mental health, schools should allow teachers more flexibility and create better work-life policies and practices.

Reflection QUESTIONS

1. Why did you become a teacher, and what keeps you motivated?

_____

_____

_____

_____

2. How does the emphasis on exams and data impact your teaching? Is there another way?

_____

_____

_____

_____

3. How do you prioritise your mental health, and what changes could improve your work-life balance?

_____

_____

_____

_____

4. What's the biggest challenge you've faced in your career, and how did you overcome it? Do you (or could you) do things differently now as a result?

_____

_____

_____

_____

CHAPTER FIVE
WHAT IF YOU LEAVE?

Vivienne's **VIEWPOINT**

Someone said to me the other day, "Now you've given up teaching", and I said, "I haven't given up! I very much consider myself to be a teacher, as I always did." It's just that I found a different aspect of teaching that fits in with the rest of my life. It fits in with my family. It fits in with having some kind of balance. I found a way through and to quote one of my fellow teachers at LWC, "This is teaching, how I always wanted it to be." I'm still a teacher, but teaching how I always wanted to teach, which is with lots of care and attention to individuals. Adapting teaching, rapport, using humour, all those things that I always did try to feature in my practice. But obviously with limited results, bearing in mind that there were 32 people to look after in every class, with multiple classes per day, plus parents, colleagues, data entry…

JM

When you say that you've left teaching, everybody interviews you about why you've left! If I'm going to summarise what made me leave mainstream teaching, here are the three main things:

The first one is bureaucracy and petty rules. The red tape and paperwork stops learning being fun. Then you've got the really daft stuff, like uniform. I'm an advocate of uniform as an equaliser for students, but I think it gets blown out of proportion. The fact that kids couldn't come to my lessons because they didn't have the right shoes on really upset me, especially when a lot of my students came from a pupil premium background, where the deprivation levels were high and they didn't have any other shoes. I had a student who was a good kid and had the right school shoes, but it had been torrential rain on the walk home from school the previous day, and he'd put his shoes on the radiator to dry, but the family didn't have enough money to put the heat on for long enough to dry them. He came in the next day in trainers and ended up in isolation for the day. When the girls went on holiday the mums would take them to get their gel nails done and they couldn't get them off, they'd sit in isolation for a day.

The second is: we've accidentally built the education system to fit one kind of person who's studious, can focus very well for an hour – sometimes two - at a time, is happy to be sat in close proximity with other people and finds it very easy to follow rules and regulations, even if they don't quite understand them. They can learn a certain way, using certain activities. But as soon as you get an outlier from that group that needs to walk around the classroom a little bit more, that needs more dynamic activities, that struggles to focus for more than 10 minutes at a time - the education system completely fails them. I'm quite an empathetic person and I honestly used to go home and cry, because the school figured out quite quickly that I was really good at teaching what they pegged as being low ability students. They weren't low ability students. A lot of them had behavioural issues, so they ended up in the lower ability class and it restricted them. I honestly used to go home, and say to my partner, "I couldn't do anything to help them, because of that red tape!"

The third thing I tend to point to is teachers who stab each other in the back to get a leg up. I was lucky to have a fantastic team - everybody was so lovely, everybody was fantastically personable but you cannot avoid the fact that it's a race to the top, and if you're not part of that race (or even if you are), you get used and abused, and you get rinsed for your work, and then they put their name on it and present it as if it's theirs. You start thinking to yourself, "Who am I doing this for? Why am I doing this? Is it for the kids, or is it for somebody else's progress reports?"

Personally, I found that I was burnt out every week because I was chasing my tail, you know, with the usual workload. Don't get me wrong - I still have quite a high workload now with all the plates that I spin in my job as a self-employed tutor, but I don't have any of the emotional stress.

SEC

It's such a fascinating job. But it can be so overwhelming; it's not for everyone and why should it be? You can leave if you don't like it once you're in and I guess if you don't like the school, try another one.

KP

It's sad when people who start out to do good with our younger generation end up feeling totally deflated by it all. You've just got to be brave and recognise that you do have the skills to do other stuff, and opportunities will come up. A lot of the work I do now is with people I had contact with before. I just didn't know that I would need them in another setting.

When in that school system, you become institutionalised into a way of working. It took me time to recognise that there are alternative ways of doing things. I spent 10 years building relationships with local families and working out what I wanted to do. I did a bit of work for an adult education charity teaching English to people that needed to get their C grades at GCSE. I taught kids at a football club who were doing a BTEC and needed to resit. It led to me working as an examiner and senior moderator. Going through the exams process as a learning provision centre could be scary, if you didn't understand the background or know how this process works. Understanding how to work a policy is scary. But I'm not scared of it, because I've done it previously. Everything has tailed neatly into this, but not because that was my plan. It just happened that way.

I think you need time out to really have a break first, though, because teaching is exhausting. If you're doing something that you don't like or it doesn't work for you, you can change it. Nothing is permanent, is it? I gave private tuition working for an adult education company. I even taught English to a business down the road from us for 12 weeks doing exam marking and moderating. Everything adds to you as a person and your skills.

Education has many facets. I work with a lot of people who aren't teachers. They're in the council working as mental health practitioners with young people and families, as part of the special educational needs team or caseworkers. Those skills you learn as a teacher are applicable to many other things. Have a look and see what's available. The civil service is full of ex-teachers because they are very good at the processes. A lot of commissioners I work with in the council are teachers. Some of them are psychologists working alongside teachers to provide support for the children's department. If you work in a school, that's all you ever think of, but there is life after teaching.

KM

In my role as headteacher, I had become increasingly frustrated by the amount of paperwork and data crunching in an education system that had become too fragmented, with different rules for academy chains and local authority schools and a distinct lack of coherence in policy. It had been building for a long time, but I still remember two occasions which proved to be a final catalyst in my decision to resign.

I was sitting in a meeting with governors and teachers discussing the arrival of a small group of new students and listening to a very enthusiastic year six teacher explain that if we really focussed on drilling in the SPAG they had missed out on, we could get them ready and close the gap – whereas to me it was blindingly obvious that our priority, our duty of care was to focus on how to integrate them into this new school setting, help them to learn to communicate confidently in their new surroundings and feel a level of safety and security socially and emotionally before forcing any academic issues. We needed to get them into a resourceful state in order to enable them to use their brains to make sense of what we were asking them to study.

The second instance was a visit I made with colleagues to observe 'best practice' at another school. The headteacher talked at me for nearly three hours, clearly very impressed with herself and the school. Sitting in her office was like visiting a bank manager. I felt myself taking on the persona of a very small, powerless child (so different from the confident, assertive leader my staff knew me as) and I hated to think that was happening to pupils at that school!

When I first left there was a period of mourning, a sort of bereavement process. Working in school communities was my whole life. But then I realised that I could still remain within the field of education, but this would give me a chance to step outside of that relatively small bubble and explore other disciplines, which is what I've done for the last eight years.

I believe that everyone should find their Ikigai – that intersection between what you love, what the world needs, what you can be paid for and what you are good at. I have certainly found mine. I would describe myself as an educationist. It runs in my blood. If we can help young people to understand how their brain works it will help us all to work from an empowerment, strengths-based perspective, rather than one where children are weak or don't measure up.

EP

I say this as somebody who bloody loves being a teacher… I love the act of teaching. I love the relationships I get to build with my students. In every school I've been in, I have found reasons to love my job – but this year has been exhausting; even without taking on a subject lead role, my whole department is more exhausted this year than they were last year (because of the workload, the increasing pressures and the problems with money that everybody's having). I think there's been a point almost every week where I've said to my husband or thought to myself, "I need a different job!"

Having Long Covid massively affected things like my salary because I can no longer work full time. It's a disability that I acquired at work because I got sick at work with Covid and there's a very high correlation between going back to work too soon, doing too much too soon and developing some form of post viral illness. Long Covid is classed as a post-viral chronic illness like ME or chronic fatigue syndrome and there's a high correlation of it affecting women (I think it's 70% women) and working in a caring profession. I have now been diagnosed with ME as well, so I could technically request less classroom time and more administrative duties to reduce my work and fatigue load. But I didn't. I just asked to go part time, because I knew that that would be more favourably received, and because my husband

and I looked at the numbers and agreed that we could afford to do that - we don't have children and we own our own home.

But I know other teachers in similar circumstances, who have been unable to go part time, because they cannot take that financial hit. I know others who have left school or are taking early retirement because they can't cope. For those who are nearing retirement: the salary for your last few years dictates what your pension is. So, if they went it would affect their pension and they can't afford that. I was looking at leaving the profession altogether if they didn't let me remain part time (temping or secretarial work, because it would be work that I could manage, and a lot of these jobs allow for hybrid working).

When I was training, it was generally thought that you should spend your NQT year and one other year at your first school so that you could make your mistakes in your NQT year and then you can work on refining things in the second year. I don't think that's actually very good advice because if the environment is incredibly toxic or really not working for you, you need to feel empowered to move if you need to.

The best way to avoid burnout - or minimise it - is making sure that you are paying robust attention to your mental health. If your self-esteem is in the toilet, then you are not going to be on the lookout for things that are burning you out. If you are feeling well in yourself mentally, then it's easy to take a step back and say, "No, this isn't OK and I'm not staying for this."

Don't be afraid to walk away. That could mean walking away from the school, or a specific situation that you're in right now. You can come back to things when you feel more able to deal with them.

SMA

The reason I've considered getting out of teaching is that a lot of things have happened that make me feel I couldn't go through that again - this is not helpful for me. So, for me: I feel like I've given this almost four years and to be honest with you, I'm almost out. My exit plan is all lined up. I'm pretty good to go.

LOD

I was at one school for the entire time I taught. I did eventually accept the position of head of languages but I was already looking elsewhere, outside of teaching. I was only doing four days a week and coping fine, but they were threatening that if I wanted to carry on with the head of department role I'd have to go up to full time, because they didn't want people in middle management being part time. I just could not see myself spending the rest of my life teaching. The constant levels of high stress would have completely killed me! It's hard in teaching to look elsewhere, without declaring your intention to leave but I was lucky because the first interview fell on my day off, so I didn't have to notify anyone of my intentions. Most people keep it secret and call in sick on the day.

I battled with the decision to leave. Should I give it another go in another school, or should I just give up on teaching? Teaching was my first job, so it was very hard to find the confidence to start applying elsewhere anyway, outside the realm of teaching. Obviously, we know that teachers have transferable skills and are incredibly resilient human beings and very, very hardworking. But there's a point where you don't quite know where to start and there's the worry about having to start at an entry level position again. I was very willing to take the financial hit to make the transition out of teaching but then I found a role with ESU, which was a fantastic fit (first as a senior officer and then as an education development manager) and I was very lucky.

ESU is a charity that supports oracy provision in school through debating competitions. These are supported by the school programme side, which helps train teachers and students in oracy through public speaking debate. My first job with them was on the education program side. This involved overseeing delivery of speaking and delivering workshops but also creating and improving resources. The transferable skill I had was the ability to plan lessons for a diverse range of needs and ages. I was in charge of assessments and training the teachers, so experience of managing a department and individual staff members and their training needs also came into my new job.

ESU prefers to employ ex teachers to fulfil their oracy roles because it is no small feat going into classrooms of 30 13-year-olds who hate being there and trying to teach them something that's often out of their depth. Previously they employed university students, who were keen debaters and public speakers, and obviously of a very high calibre and very intelligent, like Oxford and Cambridge graduates. But they couldn't cope in a classroom setting for the reasons outlined in this interview. What's needed is people with experience in the classroom who are robust in personality and resilience, and who know how to handle anything that's thrown at them. To explore the charity sector as a job after teaching is a good idea, because charities are likely to have some kind of angle within education to promote their mission and gain support.

These days there are boundaries I set that are normal outside the realms of teaching. A TOIL (Time Off in Lieu) is one of those. If I'm working an event, or I have to travel well beyond my hours, I get that time back, which is a complete godsend.

The biggest thing is that I can go to the toilet whenever I want to – that is absolutely mind-blowing when you come out of teaching! I can even take my lunch whenever I choose to, whereas I used to grab my lunch, bring it back to my desk, close my door, and turn off the lights, so I wouldn't be constantly interrupted by children in the15-minute break out of a 12-hour day.

Vivienne's VIEWPOINT

Speaking of charities: for me, ESU (Louissa's first employer outside of teaching) is a perfect addition to what I do, because I love being in the classroom and working with other teachers. It's fascinating going into different schools, meeting different groups of kids and observing the school ethos. It can be quite nerve-wracking just before you deliver a speaking or debating workshop, but then you start interacting with students, making them smile and enthusing them and remember this is something you love. There's an absence of stress because it's just a short-term gig, with no prior planning and no marking – all the nice bits!

AP

It doesn't have to be a once and for all decision either, does it? You could be a teacher who has decided to take a bit of a break for a while and do some other work, who then comes back into teaching. Absolutely. I think we should be more accepting that people do have different careers. They have portfolio careers and to move in and out of a career. You know, why wouldn't you do that?

Vivienne's VIEWPOINT

I love the idea that it doesn't have to be a forever decision, that you might decide to step away for a while if there are other things in life that are a priority for you right now. It feels like such a finality while you are grappling with such a big decision (I know it did for me) but there may be a way to reframe this situation you are in just now. Is it possible that other people have done just that – left, only to return at a time or in a setting that feels like a better fit? Just leaving that door ajar, in case you decide you might want to revisit in the future, could take some of the pressure off you right now. It is perhaps worth mentioning, as well, that people in crisis tend to catastrophise or only see the stark black and white choices, rather than the numerous shades of grey that also exist.

Reflection QUESTIONS

Many teachers leave the profession due to unfair or unrealistic policies, excessive bureaucracy, or emotional burnout. Leaving mainstream teaching needn't mean giving up entirely but could involve tutoring or working on a smaller scale, such as in an alternative provision centre. Fulfilment can be found in careers connected to education where your skills will be welcomed e.g., jobs in the charity sector, local council or civil service. You can take time out of teaching and return when it suits you – your QTS will still be valid.

1. Are there any roles still connected to education you could explore which might better fit your lifestyle and values?

   _____

   _____

   _____

   _____

2. Have you experienced burnout in your professional life, and what triggered it?

_____

_____

_____

_____

3. What are your most transferable skills?

_____

_____

_____

_____

CHAPTER SIX
HOW CAN YOU STAY?

JM

My advice for teachers on the brink of burnout would be: if it literally is a never-ending cycle of burnout, it could be the school. My experiences at different schools have been so varied. The last school I worked at had the highest workload of my career - it was beyond what I did for university, that was the case because the head of department was a workaholic, demanding the same from all her staff, so keeping up with her demands was very difficult. Often, they're a fantastic person to bounce ideas off because they've thought about things three million times before they've got on with it themselves. Unfortunately, though, she'd send an email at half past nine at night, and then be cross the next morning because you hadn't replied. I worked at another school where they didn't do bookmarking, so it could just be the school. If you find yourself constantly on the brink of burnout, a change of school might alleviate that issue. However, be careful with the questions you ask during your interview, such as bookmarking policies and how many mocks they do a year. They might start to get suspicious of you, thinking you won't be able to handle it.

But honestly, you need to think to yourself what will happen if you don't do this work. Some work is more important than others. A member of staff might ask you to get something done and make it sound compulsory, but it isn't. So, prioritise your tasks accordingly because you're more valuable to the school in a fit state of mental health than suffering in the trenches of burnout.

The quality of work produced, and teaching, increases when you're happier. So, it might mean that a very difficult thing needs to be done where you say you have not got time that week to get something done. You can do it next week and negotiate deadlines. That requires a lot of bravery, but many deadlines are actually negotiable if you dig deeper.

Let go of the fact that in your teacher training, you basically get told to make everything yourself. When you become a real teacher, you need to totally undo that mindset. You need to go in the opposite direction. Just find appropriate resources online. Take it all, and just care less because it's just so much work for so little reward.

My other piece of advice would be to put some physical activity at the top of your priority list. You have to do something to move your body outside in the sun regularly. Otherwise, cortisol builds up in your body, and you start getting ill. You need the endorphins.

Regular physical activity created a significant shift in my mental health. I found that doing some exercise in the morning worked best because by the time I got home from work, I didn't want to do it in the evening. I was exhausted; all I wanted to do was doom scroll on social media in bed to emotionally recover and wind down for sleep.

In the morning, it was just autopilot putting on my running stuff next to the bed, and by the time I got outside, I was ready to go. It set me on the right path for the rest of the day, and then stuff that usually would drag me down started bouncing off me. I was able to cope a lot better because I was making that choice for myself.

We ended up with a little running group at school - staff, not students. We ran together around the school playing fields because there were no sports activities on that day. We picked the day where the kids wouldn't be in the field. It was a really nice social thing we had together. We even applied for some funding from the school for snacks and club t-shirts because they had money in a pot for the wellbeing of staff. I pitched it to the headteacher as improving the wellbeing of his staff.

Vivienne's VIEWPOINT

When I was a secondary school teacher, I tried hard to at least incorporate regular walks into my weekly routine, but my sleep patterns were atrocious and I would regularly stay up till ridiculous hours, then get up at six a.m. and start all over again. There were days when I used sugar as a crutch to get me through. Now I am more reflective and intentional about sleep, diet, movement, and spending time outside. I play badminton, go to the gym; practise Yin yoga and meditation and I love walking my dogs and working in my garden or allotment. Whilst I'll make temporary sacrifices for an important project – like writing this book – I make sure that I build in periods of rest and recuperation after a really intensive period of work or tight deadline. Tiredness, poor diet and insufficient exercise deplete your energy and creativity supplies and affect the quality of your work.

DS

My daughter went out to New Zealand last May. She was thinking "I'm just going to quit teaching; after four years, I've had it. The demands of heads of department and leaders are just unrealistic." And I said, well, you know, give it a go anyway. So, she's gone back to the school, and she's discovered the joy by just teaching. She doesn't have to worry about any of the other stuff. Once you decide to excel at the teaching part and you find efficient, time saving ways to do it, you feel rejuvenated, and luckily that coincides with the New Zealand mindset. She's in a department of 30 English teachers, and there are 3,400 kids. They advertised for a second in department, but nobody wanted to do it. Their attitude was: why would we do that? We've got a balanced life, doing stuff we enjoy. And if that's your mindset, everything becomes easy and as a result you'll get better progress and then you will think, "Maybe I could do this for a whole department." You'll find it easier to get promoted and to make promotion manageable. So that mindset of "I'm just going to do this and enjoy it", both saves you time and promotes you.

GP

Are you in the position to meet that inspirational teacher from your own time at school? Meet with them, have a coffee, find out how human they are - it'll surprise you even now!

If you feel that you are on the brink of burnout: take a time out, step away, view it all from a distance. What could you change now to help with this? Start with a mental health day and work from there. Remember money is NOT everything, value yourself and if part time or a change in responsibility will help reduce the burnout, then explore this.

Teaching is important to me, but it is no longer what defines me - I learnt this after 10 years - now I value myself and my time. A sense of humour is crucial, as is developing great relationships with parents of the learners. I couldn't do this job without organisation, which entails lists, diaries and priority management. The firm boundaries I have set are: No work on a Friday evening or Saturday under any circumstances. I'd advise any teacher to value holidays, take time away and tell students and colleagues when you're going to be out of contact.

What I am doing now to achieve work/life balance is prioritising myself and my partner over work - we have a wedding to plan for! I accept when I'm ill or under the weather and take the time to rest and recover. I've learnt to talk to trusted friends who are NOT in my current school about how to manage situations. I love running! (And swimming, and walking). I love listening to podcasts that have humour or lifestyle… things that are going to make me smile.

EP

The best advice I was given as a teacher - which I didn't pay very much attention to at the time, but now I do (mostly) - was during teacher training. There was a whole cohort of trainee teachers across subjects, and the lecturer said, "Put your hands up if you would say that teaching is a job. Then put your hands up if you would say that you are a teacher." I put my hand up the second time. He said, "For those of you who put your hands up the second time: you are going to burn out within three years if you don't find another way of thinking of yourself, because this is a job, and it is not worth your life."

I thought, "How can you be a teacher without giving your all? It's so much more than a job." I've had to curtail other things I wanted to do - partly because of becoming ill, but also partly because that first year in teaching I just had no life. I can remember one of my best friends saying, "You used to be capable of talking about any subject eloquently and intelligently. And now all you talk about is teaching!" It is completely absorbing. You're working with other people who are in the same environment all the time. You do become institutionalised into thinking that teaching and school is everything. It really isn't.

Have friends who are not teachers, have people in your life who are not part of the profession, who are not part of the institution, who don't know when half term is, who can remind you what normal expectations are around work (apart from doctors or nurses because they also have ridiculous attitudes towards work!) Keep returning to the outside influences that can remind you what is normal.

Another tip for avoiding burnout is to not always say yes. Even if you want to appear friendly and helpful, this is not working your way up the corporate ladder, where if you take on loads of stuff now, they'll notice and give you a big promotion and you'll be made partner in five years. That is not how teaching works. If you start with yes, people will give you as much as you say you can handle. It's better to under-promise and overdeliver. If somebody asks you to do something extra, you can evaluate how much you're doing now, how manageable it feels. Is this other thing going to take a lot out of you? Find out how long you need to do this other thing for. Is it a finite project that you can learn from and recover from or is it an ongoing role?

The most useful phrase I've found recently is, "I would love to do that. What should I de-prioritise to make that happen?" You've shown willing, you've shown an interest, but you're still making it clear that you have other responsibilities. I've recently taken on a responsibility role as assistant subject leader in my department. The number of times people have said, "Could you do this thing?"

and I've asked, "Is that something that's already going on?"

"No, but we think it'd be nice to introduce a new initiative..."

"Great, I'd love to workshop that before next year. But I don't think it's feasible to try and introduce that this academic year." Or: "that would be wonderful. Do you know someone else who'd be able to take that project on?" Or: "should I drop something I'm already doing? Because, I don't have the capacity."

I am more than happy to spend a couple of hours on the phone getting theatre tickets for a one-off thing, like taking the kids to see Macbeth with David Tennant, for example. That is a worthwhile thing to be spending a brief, intense amount of time organising, and it will pay off at the other end. If it's to design a new intervention for reluctant readers in Year 9, I've just revived a previous project and found another teacher to run it. I have technically organised that, but I've not devoted loads and loads of extra energy towards it. There is merit in being smart about the amount of energy you expend, because you know your energy capacity best.

I'm not frightened of leaving. I don't want to leave teaching - I love teaching, I love my job, but it helps that if they said, "Well, if you can't do this, then we'll have to ask you to go or, we may not be able to renew your contract", if it did come down to that, I do feel I'd be able to say, "Okay that's fine. This isn't worth my life." It's a privilege that I can financially afford to do that. In some ways, having a chronic illness or disability does force you to reevaluate things.

Since becoming ill it's not so much that I've become militant, but I've certainly become a lot more aware of going, "Nope, that is past the time where I want to be working right now. You are not paying me right now, and therefore I'm not going to reply to that email, even if you send me a follow up email saying you need to get it done by tomorrow." There was an inset day a while ago, where I agreed to attend because I would have been at work. But I agreed to only attend for the number of hours I would have been working that day. Then it was time for me to go, and somebody said, "Oh, you off early, then?" And I said, "No, they stopped paying me, so I'm going home. That is the end of my working hours, and I'm done." You know what? I never got to the point before where I was being sensible and doing that. Now I get it.

When you're starting out you want to be a good teacher. You want to be a good member of the team, and if the work culture around you is, "Yeah, that's fine. I'll do five hours extra work for no extra money and no, no, it's okay - I'll arrange for someone else to pick up my children and go to their school play. It's absolutely fine - my leg's falling off, but I'll be there!" It's very difficult to buck the trend. It's also hard to see clearly, because that becomes normal behaviour and the amount of peer pressure is unbelievable. I've got a colleague who is incredibly capable and hardworking but prioritises being at home on time to see her children, because that's something that matters to her. Even though it's very far from the case, I've heard other colleagues say, "She's a bit lazy, isn't she?" No - she sets boundaries around what she's willing to do for the job and what she isn't willing to give up. So be prepared to accept the consequences for that, even if people are misunderstanding you or labelling you. If you feel safe to do so, it's also about backing up your colleagues when they aren't participating in the nonsense martyrdom culture.

There's also something to be said about how we treat new entrants to the profession, regardless of age or relevant experience. If somebody is new to the job, then they should be given the same amount of slack you would give a student who's new to a topic or a subject because they are learning. True, they're an adult, not a child, but they don't know what they're doing. And if you treat them with – frankly - the disdain and impatience that you would never do with one of your students, then you are doing a disservice to a new colleague. You are preventing someone from becoming a new colleague if you behave like that. It's very interesting to me how teacher trainees are often treated. Being frightened of their Year 9s might seem ridiculous right now but remember when you had a particular class that just got under your skin, and you were scared, and you were learning at that point. Why would you ridicule them instead of trying to help them get over it? Don't just reserve your empathy for your students – save it for yourself and for the people you work with. If you can't have empathy for yourself, you can't have it for your colleagues because you're holding yourself to a ridiculous standard that you're expecting of them as well.

Advice for new teachers: Don't expect to have to do it all by yourself and be an expert suddenly. You don't know what you don't know. Work out as quickly as you can which colleagues in your department have the capacity and the inclination to be supportive. It doesn't have to be your mentor or someone in your department, it could be somebody else who's willing to help you with the questions you think you should probably know because they were covered in your induction day four weeks ago! You need to find people, whether it's other trainees or another early career teacher, willing to answer the question that starts with, "this might sound silly, but...' Write down your 'silly" questions in a list, so you're not feeling so overwhelmed and then see at the end of the day whether any of those have been inadvertently answered by somebody else doing something or mentioning something. Then, if they're still relevant, ask them at that point.

Also, identify who you cannot ask. If you want to get things right, the temptation is to ask whoever's nearest, so that you can do it as quickly as possible. With the best will in the world, when other people are frantically busy and stressed, they will not necessarily make the time and space to do that with you. You might end up feeling even more stupid than you did in the first place, that you've made a faux pas or irritated people and the emotional side of it can really take a toll.

Particularly at the beginning, have somebody you can vent to (not necessarily in teaching), who won't ask too many questions, will find you a cup of tea or glass of wine and be there whilst you offload. That could be a therapist, that could be a friend – it could even be a dog! Just have an outlet for when it does get too much. Because it can have quite an impact on your mental wellbeing, and you need to make sure you look after that first and foremost.

When preparing your lessons, remember that the kids don't care whether the boxes on your slides are perfectly aligned. I say that as somebody who spent four hours planning each lesson to make sure everything was perfect! Particularly when you are training: some of the stuff you create will be great, but a lot won't be because you don't know what you're doing yet. If it is that great, you'll come back to revisit it later and tweak it then to make it more perfect. Just make sure it's dyslexia friendly, written with common sense and not full of flashing images!

Modelling behaviour, being authentic and having integrity is important. Children can tell when you are making it up or covering things up. You don't have to be right all the time. One of the most valuable things you can do for a child around a lesson, is to model how to accept that you're wrong and correct yourself gracefully. You must be robust in your sense of self and be able to say, "Whoops that was an error. Let's correct it," or if you don't know something: "Hey let's look that up because it sounds interesting."

Don't take yourself too seriously. I routinely take the piss out of myself – it's a part of the job I love!

Be willing to be vulnerable with your colleagues because if nobody shows any vulnerability, then everyone is terrified of showing weakness and that's no good in this job.

You also need the ability to say no to cake when there's a lot of it about!

Vivienne's **VIEWPOINT**

Switching schools could help to alleviate burnout and provide a deeper level of job satisfaction. Harness the increased energy and boost your physical and mental wellbeing through taking regular exercise and getting enough sleep. Treat teaching as a job, not your identity. Use existing teaching resources to save time and reduce stress. You can always tweak them if needed but don't be too much of a perfectionist. Look for a mentor and supportive colleagues at school and maintain your non-teaching connections to help maintain a healthy perspective.

Reflection QUESTIONS

1. Where, when and how often could you incorporate physical exercise into your day?

_____

_____

_____

_____

2. Who are your key supporters and how can you strengthen these relationships?

_____

_____

_____

_____

3. Are there ways you could streamline your planning by using ready-made resources, or building a bank of

materials you can use again?

_____

_____

_____

_____

4. Do you admit to mistakes, accepting them as part of the learning process and how can you be a positive role model to students in this area?

_____

_____

_____

_____

CHAPTER SEVEN
WHY WON'T THEY BEHAVE, AND WHAT COULD YOU TRY INSTEAD?

Vivienne's **VIEWPOINT**

Behaviour management is such a huge topic that it needs to be in its own book and - if the shelf in my study currently groaning under the weight of many of the best-known behaviour bibles is anything to go by – many people have reached the same conclusion. I asked the experts in this book for their views and you may just find some valuable nuggets here to add to your tool belt of techniques. I think it's important to avoid copying others but adapt the advice that makes sense to you and develop your own teaching style. Ideally, you will also be constantly reflecting on and improving your behaviour management.

I know someone whose placement mentor had a Year 7 class and they were incredibly badly behaved for the mentor, who was a very able teacher. He had his own funny ways of dealing with them, but she couldn't ever get a grip on what to do with them herself because the way he dealt with behaviour wasn't really working for him either. In another school she taught in, she learnt just never to ask advice from her head of department because they were like chalk and cheese so she couldn't have followed their advice anyway - it was so specific to the other person's personality and mannerisms and also at odds with the school's own behaviour policy.

SEC

When you train how to train teachers, or when you're being trained yourself, there is that temptation to go into the model that the mentor teaches in initially, until you find your own feet. If every time you have someone going into the classroom to give you advice, they do so from the perspective of their own teaching styles, you can't apply it because they're not your teaching style so it doesn't work. Instead, I would look at current pedagogy and research. I would ask other people I felt were maybe a little bit more like me how they dealt with it. If you do decent coaching as a mentor, the mentee themselves is solving their own problem by talking it out.

Don't take anything personally from a student in terms of

behaviour; it is very unlikely to be personal. Try and support them by getting to the root of why they're angry or why their behaviour is happening. Reward in public, reprimand in private. Don't raise your voice. You don't need to. And be kind. Because if your working environment isn't kind or you can't be kind, you need to not be doing the job. The minute you can't do that, you've lost your soul.

The Kit Messenger 'Curious, not Furious' course that we did at the University of London has changed the way that I manage a classroom. I now no longer challenge students at the beginning of a lesson. If they're late, I just say, 'Carry on, sit down, and we'll have a discussion at the end." What those students do when they come in and behave like that is rarely personal. It's rarely you that they're raging against - you're not the machine. They're raging against the machine itself. Within that 'curious to furious' approach the most helpful bit (including teacher to teacher) is that what's the matter may be something fundamental that you don't know about. There was a very well-built boy who was constantly being told off for not wearing his blazer, but it turned out that the largest school blazer didn't fit him. He was constantly being told off and feeling isolated and different and the curious not furious mechanism allowed us to find out the real reason why - he wasn't being deliberately difficult at all. That problem was quite easily solved, but it is that drilling down into what those individuals are. That's a pastoral issue in many respects, but we very rarely have time within a classroom to find out what would be causing a student distress and what would be causing an individual joy. Because it suddenly clicks, doesn't it? But it doesn't happen very often nowadays.

Quite often now I will not move until there's silence. I now say,

"This is about you. This is about your response. This is about your level of self-control. You can stop the person next to you talking, you can get yourselves ready for safe, respectful working. I am not your parents. You need to find this within yourselves", and I do it repeatedly until the message gets through. I've recently picked up a class who've had a lot of cover and I've gone right back to basics with them because they were behaving like small children, frankly. Now they're cheering when I walk through the door, because they know they needed those boundaries. They needed those levels of security where they know what they've got to do. The other teachers that I'm sharing with are doing the same thing and the students are happier and much more secure. However, for those students whose parents either can't be present - either physically or intellectually - or whose parents who don't value education themselves it's more of a challenge. If the parent is totally disengaged from their child's education, that might be as a result of their own education. If they've had a poor experience themselves, they can be genuinely scared of teachers or headteachers, so you have two battles to fight! It does put a lot of pressure on, particularly on the new entry teachers because they are having to balance more things and it feels sometimes like co-parenting! It is not untrue that our roles as social workers and counsellors are significantly higher. There won't be a single day in my teaching week where I don't have to take myself and another student out of class or to Heads of House at some point, to support them emotionally. Not necessarily for behaviour, but because something traumatic has happened or they're upset with their crimes. I'm not going to pretend I don't have 'You can talk to me' written on my forehead! I'm happy that they see me in that way - and staff too. It adds another layer of responsibility though, and sometimes I've finished my day's work, and then they'll be waiting to ask my advice, or just download!

Vivienne's VIEWPOINT

When I first started teaching, I was too polite to wait for silence. I'd try and talk over the chatting, hoping that they would catch on and bring the conversation to a close. Now I realise that this creates an impression and feeling of weakness or lack of control, which is counterproductive for both the teacher and students. I state my expectations clearly and confidently and hold my ground.

AP

I think the pressure when I first started teaching in that first school was all around behaviour management because there wasn't a whole school approach. You either had a reputation that went before you and that meant that you didn't have any problems, or you had to establish yourself, so a lot of my energy in that first year went into trying to establish good relationships with classes that I was teaching. I managed that with every class bar one - a Year 8 class that I only taught for 45 minutes a week, the last lesson of the day on Tuesday afternoon. They said I could teach silent reading, so you can imagine how that went... Every week I tried to think of something different to do with them. But the school was kind of led against the children, so the staff room was a place of sanctuary and a lot of the language in the staff room was about battlegrounds. You'd come into the staff room, and it was like Relief at Mafeking! No children were allowed in and then you'd be off to 'fight the good fight again'!

The job's the same whether you're teaching 16-year-olds or 6-year-olds. It's all about the relationship you build, the presence that you have, the way in which you can convey the learning situation for the youngsters. Listening, engaging with them, making meaning. I think it's the same working with adults to be honest.

Behaviour management is about creating a culture of mutual respect. When you can do that, and when everybody in the room feels that they're safe then you can do amazing things with the class of children. It's all to do with building and sustaining relationships and making sure they're respectful relationships. Because children will have bad days and they'll act out. But if they feel humiliated as a result , that could take months to repair. So, it's really about how to keep everybody feeling safe, even if they're having a bad day. You also need a whole school approach because if that's not there, then you've got to recreate it every single time you step into a classroom. And that's very hard work. In that first school it was possible to do because they kind of reinvented themselves as a class depending on who was teaching them, and they developed an expectation of me. I'm wary of the whole school approach that requires everybody to deal with everything in the same way. You need to allow for individual circumstances and individual children. There still needs to be room for the teacher to be able to respond in the way that's best or they think is best. If it's all about policy and adherence to policy, then it all becomes quite factory-like, if we're not careful - quite quickly.

GP

Silence is more powerful, effective and makes more impact than shouting.

DS

I never prioritised classroom behaviour until later in my career. My perception is that a male teacher will typically have a classroom persona – a kind of identity they take into the classroom, whereas a female teacher will be much more their authentic self. And I couldn't get the persona bit. I just wanted to be my authentic self, and I knew that let me down in the sense I was too enthusiastic, too excitable, and therefore that made me unpredictable; which meant that behaviour at any given time might be brilliant, or it might be terrible because kids would spot the lack of consistency. I was too stubborn to change my personality or adopt a persona in the classroom - I've just got to be myself and work out how I can get better behaviour given my failings as a teacher. My techniques now revolve around the student. If the students know that what they do matters, then they're much more likely to invest time in it, so the visualiser is a key thing to use. If I'm talking to or training teachers and using a visualiser, their instinct is to just go round and find some really good bits of work and put those under but I say, "No. That is just like asking for volunteers, it gives permission to everyone else in the class to just not work." You need a random system for questioning. I always use lollipop sticks. This random system tells kids, "I'm not picking on you. This is just the way I do business. This is the way we look at work and give feedback." It's transformative. If I've got the naughtiest kid in the class, and their book gets picked up and put under the visualiser, they know that there's nothing personal in that, and I'm not humiliating them in any way; they suddenly learn that I get really excited when someone's made a mistake. "This is where I get to earn my money because I can actually teach you something!" I share that excitement with them. Within just a few weeks, your bottom set are desperate to get their stuff under the visualiser. "Give me some attention, Sir. Give me some help!"

Be explicit about your criteria. Then they can clearly see when you're praising them, that it's not bogus praise. "You've met these criteria, which I said is really good. Fantastic." So, it becomes genuine and it's very easy to build great relationships with your class that way. The other thing I'll use the lollipops for is cold call questioning. I'll only ever go to a volunteer if I'm asking a question about stuff I've never taught. It's legitimate to go to other kids' expertise, but all the other times I ask questions, if it's about stuff I've taught: lollipop sticks every time. That means every single kid thinks, "It's going to be me. I'm going to have to pay attention here!" You can make that much more efficient if you do some turn and talk. I'll frequently have 20 to 30 second discussions where kids clarify ideas with each other, then that maximises the opportunity. They'll be thinking about your work and a short time limit keeps them on task. They don't mess about and they know, "the lollipop stick's coming, I'm going to be called so I'll be on task."

The final thing I use for behaviour is the timer. Never do any activity in class without a time limit and the time limit is probably 25% of what a normal teacher would set. That dramatically increases the pace that kids work at and also that I work at because you discover "Oh crikey that thing that used to take 10 minutes: I can now literally do in two and I never knew!" Having the time limit also keeps everybody honest, especially the teacher. You know how teacher time is. I observe a lot of lessons, and this is what I see: "You've got four minutes to do this" and at eight minutes I'm looking at them and they're still doing it! Misbehaviour happens when kids have got time to misbehave. If they don't have the time, they'll do the task and it's really easy for you as a teacher. You say, "Right. My time limit's up. I've been circulating the class. I can see lots of you haven't finished. I'm going to extend it by one minute." The kids are saying, "What a lovely teacher!" rather than "Jeez, we only had three minutes to do this!"

Vivienne's VIEWPOINT

Using a timer and maintaining the pace of the class has certainly helped me to control behaviour in unruly classrooms. My first instinct had been to wait until the stragglers caught up, so that nobody got left behind, but this resulted in the students who finished on time getting bored and restless and increased the chance of them playing up.

SG

Behaviour management can be challenging. Remember they are only kids, which is what we always forget when what we see in front of us is people who are judging us, who are wild, who have a massive attitude. It's so easy to forget that we are the adults, to completely lose sight of our experience, mastery, expertise or knowledge, whereas this student is only 13 years old.

Assert yourself; you can be a very warm person, a warm teacher whilst still being very strict. Create a safe environment. Be consistent. It took me a long time to understand that if you're prepared to stop your lesson to address the behaviour before finishing your lesson, then you can start having control, then you can teach properly; you can never teach properly if there is no control because no one can concentrate. Address the behaviour first. You can finish the rest of the lesson later. It's not the end of the world. If you don't address it now, it will go mental and it will be really hard to go back to zero.

Make sure you have clear expectations from the beginning. "The rules explain what I want. If you don't follow them this is what's going to happen." Do not deviate from the rules and treat everybody equally. I never discuss or negotiate because I found that students are brilliant at saying, "But so and so in maths does this," or whatever.

I had this one Year 11 who hadn't done the homework, then he was not working properly, then he was on his phone. I lost it. I told him to get out of the classroom. When he returned, I said, "Do you want to talk about it after school today or tomorrow? But we are going to talk about what happened today," and he agreed to come after school. We had a really nice conversation and I said, "I'm going to apologise first for shouting at you. I lost it. I shouldn't have shouted. I apologise, but you need to understand what took me to that level. You didn't have your homework; you weren't paying attention and you were using your phone. Then you answered me back. Do you understand my point of view?" He said, "Yes, Miss. I understand." I explained that he would be the one ending up with the sanction, so we had to avoid this happening in the future. We reached an excellent agreement, which I could refer back to in the future. There is respect there, understanding has been established and the responsibility is shared. Build on the relationship, because you can show him how to resolve conflict as well.

You can really assert yourself as a powerful figure if you need to. If someone is really angry, you need to temporarily remove them from the class. Sometimes even when they come back to class, they're not ready. You are not going to get through to someone if they are still very angry. They're focusing on their own perspective and not ready to listen yet. So be realistic about when you're going to be able to get through to them.

Be the bigger person. Show them what you expect from them. If you are not prepared to apologise for what you've done wrong or explain calmly or agree on something with them then you're not doing your job as a teacher and showing them how. Some of the kids don't have this at home. You might be the only person in their life who actually shows them how to deal with their own impulse control. It's about establishing the boundaries very clearly, apologising if you've made a mistake and being a good role model.

Some kids can be very intimidating, but you can put things into perspective and take control. This kid is showing off or doesn't know how to behave. It's very hard for him to control himself, very hard. He stands up. He's very restless. Am I going to shout at him? No. Obviously that won't work because this boy is completely wild. So, I use a different approach. I tell him very quietly and clearly what I want from him. It doesn't always work, but what I've noticed is that it takes him time, so I give him time to settle down. I'm guessing he doesn't get that at home. Sometimes he works really hard for 10 minutes and then he stands up and says, "Miss, I can't do any more. I need to go to the quiet room" and I acknowledge his effort and let him go.

A boy was calling out across the class the other day and the others were responding. I said, "Today guys, we need to help X. It's more difficult for X to control himself and he's trying very hard. You need to help him as well, or he's going to get into trouble. If he is your friend, you need to make sure that you support him. I want you to ignore him in class but when you are in the playground, he's your friend. If you don't, you will have the sanction with him." I tried to make them understand that we are all together to support each other and he is not doing this on purpose. There is a background to this and whatever it is, we need to make sure that he is part of the class, whilst helping him to focus on the work.

I think in our school, behaviour is getting better because before everybody was doing whatever they wanted, and the policy was not

KIND WORDS FOR TIRED TEACHERS

clear. Now we have very clear displays in every classroom and parents and kids are aware. It's so much easier and it also takes it away from just you being mean, to: "It's not my fault. We all have to work by these rules. I'm doing my job, I'm not the one making the rules but they're there to make sure we can learn."

KP

When I set up LWC, what surprised me in a really good way was that you would have thought there'd be lots of behavioural issues within the centre because I'm assuming their previous behaviour at school was a way of expressing an inability to work in that setting. We have very few behavioural issues at all and even then, that behaviour hasn't really been that challenging. I think it's because each student knows they have a key adult that they're working with who's got their back. They're not expected to talk to people if they don't want to. If they're feeling as though they can't manage today, they're not going to be told, "You must come in, you need 100% attendance!" They feel a bit more relaxed and safer. There's no need for them to act out because their needs are being met. They approach the relationship with the teacher very differently and we teachers can adapt more readily to suit the student, which you can't do in a class of 30 people. Even in some specialist schools, where they have much smaller classes of five, we've had students who've found those environments quite challenging.

Working individually with a student is a privilege and a challenge for the teacher, but in a good way. It is all about relationship building. I'd like to think that any adults my children work with will want to have a positive relationship with my own children. They're in mainstream school, in a class of 32 and they seem happy - it works for them. The difference here is that our learners have all hidden in the back of classrooms or walked out of classrooms or not even managed to enter in the first place through heightened anxiety. They are hypervigilant and constantly on the lookout for the next thing that's going to sweep them off their feet, so our space and our teachers will try to reduce that for them in order to give them a positive learning environment.

KM

I've learnt so much from studying executive functioning and developing the 5C Need Scales, which helps people identify when and where their struggles occur and what conditions help them to be at their 'brain best'. Briefly, these can be boiled down to: feeling comfortable (including preventing sensory overload); connected with others; that they count; that they are capable and have a measure of control. I haven't worked with a single young offender (through my consulting for Sussex Police) who didn't have significant differences with their executive functioning processes. It goes to prove my point that so much of 'behaviour' is unmet needs and missing skills. I don't believe so much in intervention in schools as a whole school approach, which helps everyone involved – from teachers to kids to their families and anyone else supporting them - to understand how their brain works. This fundamental understanding of processing should come even before metacognition works on how they learn.

I'm excited that we now have a government that appears to be listening to schools (something that is actually quite rare!) It looks like they will be guided – at least to some extent - by research for the Teach

First "Belonging Schools" report, which examines how secondary schools approach and practise inclusion. It's clear from looking at the data - not just the curriculum - but giving children a much bigger sense of autonomy that's not tokenistic. We've got to be great facilitators, great teachers and great educators but I think it's about walking with them on the journey of doing it, too.

We've got to look at neuro inclusion now and what that can look like in the next 20 years. We know so much more about the brain now than we did 15 years ago, but we haven't really changed what we're doing. We could go into schools to look at to what extent they are managing to work and include children who have got a different brain profile. How can we all support them with that? Let's all work together. Every child (even the ones who are managing) should have psychoeducation to understand how brains work, where they learn to understand each other better but also what different needs they might have, how they can self-advocate. The trouble is that because they are being 'done to' so much, they don't take responsibility. These are the kind of adjustments you get in the workplace as an adult. Rather than judgement and fear of getting things wrong, we can all work on this together and try to create the best education system. Of course, academic results matter but we want to keep the focus on people becoming learners in the wider sense of the word – understanding the material, being able to focus, being able to remember, being able to process stuff. All of these are to do with executive functioning and some children find that difficult because they process things differently; some children will struggle and need additional coaching, without making them feel like they are being inconvenient. But there isn't a child on this planet that wouldn't benefit from doing some work on executive functioning and building their attention and memory.

I said to a school the other day, "What's your biggest resource?" They answered, "The teachers". I said, "What is the other huge resource? The children! Help them to understand the brain, and then to become coaches, and you've just created a massive tool!"

Vivienne's
VIEWPOINT

Set clear rules and apply them fairly. Bear in mind that misbehaviour could signal stress, neurodiversity or unmet needs and consider underlying circumstances. Tools like timers and random questioning can help to maintain classroom order. Show students how to handle conflicts calmly. Students behave better when they feel safe, valued and included.

Reflection QUESTIONS

1. What are <u>your</u> behaviour management strategies? Are they clear and easy to follow?

    _____

    _____

    _____

    _____

2. Does your school's behaviour policy support or challenge you?

    _____

    _____

    _____

    _____

3. Which additional structured tools and techniques could you employ in the classroom to maintain focus and order?

    _____

_____

_____

_____

4. How do you model respectful conflict management for students?

_____

_____

_____

_____

5. How can you adjust your strategies to better support neurodiversity and shift from anger to understanding?

_____

_____

_____

_____

CHAPTER EIGHT
WHAT ELSE MIGHT WORK?

AP

Advice for trainee teachers and new teachers

There is so much to learn when you first start teaching. With any initial teacher training programme, you're only going to take in a little bit of it because you've got so much to assimilate in terms of recognising yourself as someone different, because when you become a teacher, you're sort of an actor on the stage, aren't you? There's so much feedback you have to deal with, which is your interaction with the rest of the room, your interaction with the young people. How are they taking on what you're saying? Are they listening to what you're saying? Can you get their attention, and when you've got their attention, can you say something that's worth them being engaged with? Can you match tasks to capacity to learn? I mean that's a huge thing - planning tasks that are going to have enough challenge in them for the youngsters to really get hold of. So, when you first start teaching it's: "How can I think about what I might do to keep this group occupied, let alone can I give them things that are going to stretch their intellectual capacity as well?" There's so much to learn! I do think the majority of that first learning takes place in the classroom, face-to-face with classes. Also, I think there's no substitute for having a brilliant mentor. You can have a great mentor that makes a massive difference. But that's why at the Chartered College, we don't expect people to begin chartered study until they've been teaching for three years. Because we think it takes you three years really to get yourself settled, to get your feet under the table to know what you're doing, and then once you've started thinking, "Oh, I know what I'm doing around here", probably that's the time we need to disrupt what you're doing and say, "There are other ways of approaching this!"

It's not about you, it's about them. How are they? How are they managing to learn or are they? How does it feel to be in your classroom? Is your classroom somewhere that every child knows they're valued and they're recognised for who they are and encouraged to do their best, or is your classroom frankly a bit of a Wild West? Because if that's how it feels to you, it's a Wild West for them as well; where no one necessarily feels they can speak up or say anything without being jeered at. Creating that environment where everybody feels safe is crucial.

But it's also about making learning meaningful. I learnt so much when I did my master's at Cambridge. I was very fortunate. I took time to have a career break, had our two daughters and then I was able to study at Cambridge for a period of two years to do a master's degree. I don't know how people do that and teach full time! As it was, I remember writing an essay (or trying to write an essay) with my two-year-old daughter grabbing my leg. This essay was all about how in the early years it's important for adults to scaffold play and I was going, "Get off, go play. Get off, go away. Because I need to write this essay on how to support children's play!"

During that course, I was fortunate to have excellent lectures, to read a lot and to reflect deeply how children make meaning in learning situations and the difference between what we think we are conveying and what's actually received.

When you first start out teaching you believe that if you tell them this, this is what they're going to learn. However, they may not be listening, and it might mean something totally different to them and they might not make the connections that you think they're going to make. Learning is all about making connections. The job of teaching and learning is endlessly fascinating and difficult, and incredibly complex. If you've got it down to the art of it feeling simple, you've probably got it wrong. You must remain humble and open to other ways of doing things, to listening and to allowing children to surprise you. That's fundamental, because if you stop allowing children to surprise you then you predetermine what they're capable of, just because of what it tells you on a data sheet...

Developing a relationship with parents is crucial. When I was a head teacher, we used to have 15-minute parent consultations (daytime or evening, whenever was convenient for the parent) where the child gave a presentation to their parents and their teacher, and I was present. We had to limit the number of slides due to time constraints, so it was a welcome slide, a slide on their challenges, one of their successes and then things they were going to work on in the future. It was very successful. The children were so proud to talk about what they were doing. The teachers would illustrate what the children were talking about and say, "Well, here's this piece of work on this topic." Or they might say, "I think you're being a bit hard on yourself, saying that you are not able to construct a story, because look at this story you've written!" The parents were almost universally thrilled and quite taken aback by what their children could do. I was able to see the relationship between the child and their teacher, their teacher and the parents, the child and the parents. There was no hiding place for me either. If we all agreed that we needed to find books in the library about wizards and we hadn't done anything by the next time we met, I was as culpable as the teacher! I was also quality assessing what was going on as well, so I didn't need to do formal monitoring (I didn't do classroom observations). In that 15-minute meeting I could see the children's work, I could see what the children were enjoying about their work, what they were finding difficult. I could see the teacher's relationship with the child. There was a tremendous amount there and the parents were involved in that as well, in a very respectful way; the whole essence of the meeting was that we were all there together because the child was the most important person in the room, and we were there to collectively try and help them learn. It wasn't the case of home versus school, or school versus home or who's doing the best job, as those parent consultations quite often become.

I try not to tell people what to do. I try to encourage people to think about what they are doing in a different way. When I'm working with a group of headteachers, for example, I say, "Think about the school you've left behind - or the school you know best, and then think about whose classroom you'd want to be learning in if you were a child…probably it's somewhere that you know you would be understood and trusted and that the teacher would know who you were and would expect high things from you. It's not going to be the neatest classroom necessarily, but it will be the classroom where you are the one who is recognised for who you are. That's what matters." When I was a headteacher, I could walk around my school for half an hour and gauge what was going on. If you don't know what's happening or how your school's running, then you're becoming an administrator. And I don't think then that you're there to support your staff when something happens - when parents want to come and complain or ask about what's going on. How do you know if you haven't been involved?

I think if you've got an ethos where there are certain values that everybody stands by, then you can individually teach in a very different way but you can still subscribe to the fact that "we don't shout at children in this school", for example. I just don't like the idea of conformity, where everybody's doing the same thing at the same time, in the same way. I don't think there's any evidence to say that makes things better. I was speaking to someone a couple of weeks ago. Her school had been taken over by a multi-academy trust and she'd been told that all the lessons had to be taught in a particular way, using particular slides and if they wanted to amend any of the slides, they had to apply to London. Isn't that awful? The children had to copy down chunks of stuff from the slide into their exercise books as a way of checking that's what had been taught and how it had been taught. So as a school, you are giving the message that you don't trust your teachers but also that you don't have any understanding of high-quality pedagogy either, do you? I just told her to leave! I just said, "There are other schools. There are 25,000 schools - go and find another one! Quickly!"

LOD

When I first started, the tips that were given to me were just like, "Keep going. It will get better. You can do it", and that's not helpful, because what if it never does get better? The best advice I was given was to have 5 or 10 minutes' football viewing at the end of every lesson if they had behaved and worked hard, and to use that as an incentive – or they could forfeit a minute of football if they hadn't. It actually worked very well! 10 minutes of The Simpsons in Spanish also went down well sometimes!

One of the things I started to implement whilst I was head of department was to have a bank of year by year topic resources, so when a member of my team was off they wouldn't have to set cover. It's ridiculous having to set cover before seven o'clock in the morning when you're ill.

Vivienne's **VIEWPOINT**

Despite wreaking havoc with sleep patterns and creating perfect breeding grounds for anything from colds to Covid (in a heated hall, with many unmasked parents at close range, incidences of illness always seemed to rise), I always enjoyed parents' evenings. More accomplished colleagues would be able to quickly glance at the class statistics and make pertinent comments about progress and reading age and I usually made notes about the key things to discuss for each pupil which was, as usual, not time-effective for me but worked well in that our short discussion would be positive and meaningful. For me, what seemed best was to have a marked recent piece of work to discuss. I know as a parent myself that I was always intrigued to see my children's work and I found as a teacher it always spoke volumes in terms of current effort, progress and skills still to work on. We always teach the students to 'Show, not tell' and this neat, painstaking little masterpiece or shoddy torn page was sometimes more eloquent than I could be! It was, for me, a great way to connect and enlist support from home (particularly for those students with challenging behaviour), as well as a chance to give students and families a boost and renewed enthusiasm.

JM

Kids are important, obviously, everyone prioritises the students above everything else. You do it for the kids, that's why people are teachers, not for the money. Any work you do should never really be just for the benefit of the school.

The daft things that you think the kids don't want to do, they probably do. I had a real boy-heavy Year 9 class that were renowned for being unruly. It was often chaos, but it was organised chaos, and we had fun. I discovered they like singing a song about the reactivity series. I'd say, "Shall we sing a song? Who here wants to go back to primary school because it's way better than secondary school? Well, what did you do in primary school? You sang songs. Thank you. So get up. And we're going to sing this song together!" They're trying to be cool. But they're just kids. I could have given them a worksheet, and they would probably have got on with it. But they are just kids at the end of the day, and they do want to do the fun stuff that often requires less planning.

Design is always great when I incorporate drama or any interactive element with them. I could have spent hours making a worksheet for them, and made them do it, but I'd have been more on my behaviour management, and have to spend that time to make it, to print it, to get them to glue the stupid sheet in and cut it to whatever. But it's so much easier just to put on YouTube and get them to sing a song with you, and then to write something up about it later. It's just so much easier this way, and no one really teaches you how to properly streamline your planning.

People stress about having PowerPoint slides the right colour, but it just doesn't matter. The kids don't care. And I think some teachers spend so much time poring over little things that don't actually matter because they've been told it matters by another member of staff. Without sounding uncaring, you need to care less about certain aspects. And oh my God, stop making resources yourself! Just go on TES. There's so much for free. There are so many websites like Twinkl that will just do stuff for you, and there are so many games that you can play. One game I love playing with my students is called 'Crack the Circuit', and it forces them to figure out how series and parallel circuits work. I could spend a full lesson, mind-numbingly teaching them the rules about it, and then getting them to faff about with diagrams and stuff. But when we start getting into a competition and we play Crack the Circuit on the big board, I end up with my kids screaming at me because they are so engaged, so involved. No - you don't need to reinvent the wheel. Half of it's already out there for you. Just go for more simplicity.

SG

In order to mark efficiently and quickly, you already need to be very clear on your success criteria and that's what helps. My marking tip is to have a very detailed and comprehensive marking scheme in the paper. For example, when marking a paragraph we have two categories – content and language. Is the content relevant? Did you add your own opinions or specific target vocabulary? Did you include the correct tenses, time markers, classifiers, connectives, etc? So you've already got the criteria, you've already got the tick boxes. Then highlight the ones that you need to include in order to improve the paragraph and then maybe a comment box to say 'good', or 'more revision needed', or 'excellent - happy face!' This is something I introduced because I think it saves a lot of time and it's something comprehensive to the student, rather than just copying and pasting the mark scheme we use as teachers to mark the exams. We can refer to that ourselves to arrive at the mark, of course. But this is an effective way to give students your expectations and feedback that they can easily understand. It's also a powerful way to demonstrate your students' progress, which can assist you with your career progression. All teachers within that department have bought into that system, which standardises the system and provides consistency across all classes. When the head of department does their analysis, it is also much more useful.

I think in order to survive in this job you have to be strong enough to identify and say no to the nonsense, because there's a lot of nonsense that we feel guilty about e.g. Progress Eight. At the start of the year your head of department tells you that your progress is negative and your class has got two grades below other subjects. What happened? What did you do? You feel guilty. Obviously, you're a bad teacher. Maybe you have a higher percentage of low ability children. Maybe the student didn't turn up to the exam, or they only did part of the exam, or they were absent the whole year, but these just sound like excuses!

You do need to be accountable, though. My advice (when it comes to feeling more confident in that tough conversation with your line manager about progress, when it comes to the parents and when it comes to why they didn't get better grades) is to be quite methodical and record everything, then it's all there. You are playing a political game in a way. You are saying, well, I know that a lot of these students were absent. Attendance is one of the biggest indicators of how well a student will do. You can point out that you put all the lessons on Google Classroom for them to access from home and sent them a link; you contacted the parents on this date and here is the email exchange; on parents' evening you raised your concerns again, to make sure the student was on board with the work...in a way, it's a shame that you have justify yourself, but it's good insurance for you. Also, in having to show that evidence of the support you've offered, it's also reminding you what you need to do in order to do your job well and you can be content with what you've done.

It's so easy to let work or worries about school eat into your free time. You think about the problem in the car, when you get home and you don't sleep very well. The question I always ask myself is, can I actually do something about it? And if I can do something about it, is it going to make a difference? Ask yourself these two questions and if you say no to either, you must disconnect. You must think about something else. You must do something else. You must put everything in the school bag, zip up the bag and put it away. I give myself a certain amount of time to prepare my lessons etc and then I refuse to work when I go home after school during the week. Do your work at school. And then go home. At the weekend I may spend half a day planning, maybe more if I am marking mocks or assessments but I try to get most things done at school and then switch off.

DS

I couldn't teach without a visualiser now. My daughter's teaching English abroad. The first thing we did was to buy the best visualiser we could get her. She's the only teacher in a school of 3,400 kids with a visualiser. It just makes teaching so easy then, to make your feedback relevant in the moment to everyone in the classroom. Your written feedback is rarely acted on in the way that you expect by the students; they manage to misunderstand what you've written or ignore it. Do feedback live in the classroom, and then say, "OK, you've got five minutes to act on this feedback I've given the whole class and then I'm going to take a couple of books in at random, to see how that feedback has resulted in improvements." Every kid in the class is thinking, "Oh my God. He's gonna pick me!" They'll do their best to improve and then you can also measure how well your feedback has landed by getting the books and putting them on the visualizer again and you might think, "Oh no, my explanation must have been poor about this point. OK, I'll try and rectify that now with this book", and so on. But kids get the feedback exactly when they need it. And as a teacher, you can work out whether you're having an impact, or whether you were rubbish at that moment, which, let's face it, a lot of the time we are! But you can correct it straight away.

I used to take two shirts into work because everything was such high energy - I planned everything and I threw everything I had into it. I ended up uncomfortably sweaty, so I'd change into another shirt! But the longer I taught, the more I realised that if I wanted to be efficient, I needed to find ways where things became automatic. As head of department, I realised that if I got my best teachers to plan a sequence of lessons for a particular topic, those plans would be much better than I could do on my own or a single teacher could do on their own. Once you've got those lessons, they're easy to tweak if you need to. But if you don't want to, it doesn't matter because they are already excellent. In order to give everybody autonomy, get them jointly planning so everyone's involved in the planning of those lessons or resources. But you also need a time in which you review it, so that people don't feel locked into something that might not work for them. If I were head of department now, I'd have a compulsory phase where every teacher in my team would have one unit to experiment with. Then they would report back on the results, because that's the only way you find out the stuff that works even better, or the stuff that doesn't work at all. If you've got a passion for doing X, and you do X all the way through and students get worse results, then you have to face up to X being personal preference that is damaging the kids; that's a much better way to improve your practice than have somebody come into your lesson and say "I don't like X".

What if the teacher themselves feels they can't achieve? Well, I guess what I'd say is: when you scratch beneath the surface, every teacher goes into teaching to make a difference. You know, even if 80% of it was "I want the holidays," the other 20% is, "I want to make a difference." The easiest way to be motivated that way is to measure the impact of what you do.

My daughter's in her fourth year and she struggled initially because of leadership teams, leadership decisions, pointless admin tasks - all the kind of rubbish around making your life more difficult in the classroom - and she was ready to give up. I trained her to measure the impact of current teaching. Luckily, her main degree was psychology, with a huge amount of research, so it was easy to convince her to set up little experiments in class (which you can do yourself). Ask yourself: what would be the impact of me getting rid of the PowerPoint and turning my lesson, my unit of work, into a booklet? What would be the impact of putting models in the booklet and teaching from the model? Well, it's quite easy to set up and assess or use the existing assessments to then measure the impact of that after four weeks. You'll suddenly see the impact you're having and you can then pick and choose to do more of what is having a positive impact and a rationale for doing less of that which is having a negative impact.

So, let's imagine: (this is what my daughter had) there was a top-down instruction of what you had to do with marking - in books- and I said, "OK. Well, let's see if we could stick to the letter of the law, but we get the kids to do that marking." She came to the method where she'd give three pieces of feedback to every piece of work, but it was to the whole class. The kids then had to interpret that feedback and do something to their work to change it. And she found that meant she didn't have to do any marking at night, but it also met the letter of the law that the school gave. So, they would self-mark and I mean the great thing about that is: as soon as kids self-mark, you see how far they've understood your feedback. And usually because kids are novices, they will misunderstand your feedback. I mean, that's their default. And as teachers we tend to think well, I've given the right feedback. Therefore, I've done my job. If you experiment, you think, "No, my job isn't to get or give feedback. My job is to make sure the kids get better." If you're always looking for that, your teaching will constantly improve, and you will end up getting rid of lots of fluffy, time-consuming stuff.

From experience, you become liberated, you get more efficient, and you realise that by working less hard you actually get better results. That was the premise of the "Slightly Awesome Teacher". You don't have to be awesome to get awesome results from your kids. You just have to focus on some key things. The reason I mentioned my daughter is that I have never visited her classroom or seen her teach, but a 20 minute conversation once every week or every fortnight has been such an easy way to make her a highly effective teacher. She has always got the top progress even from day one. She converted from psychology to be an

English teacher. No one would give her a job as an English teacher in Wales because she didn't have an English degree, so she ended up teaching health and social care and she immediately got better results than the head of department. After two years, she didn't want to do health and social care anymore, so she had to move to another school, and she taught A-level psychology and she immediately got record results. She's a good teacher, but she didn't have to be brilliant (she couldn't have been in her first three years of teaching – that's impossible) but just by adopting the kinds of techniques that I'm talking about, and in particular, that idea of measuring how the kids are responding, made it so much easier for her to get great progress from students.

I believe in marking as you teach, if at all. Now (apart from assessments, which you have to mark) I would never mark a book. And I couldn't teach without a visualiser now. . The books are a record of the kids' learning journey. But if I give verbal feedback and they interpret it and then try something different based on my feedback, that is still a measure of their learning journey. The impact is measurable. When Ofsted come in, these books will tell a story they can understand.

Well, I haven't got good tips for resisting the calorific department treats that come out on a regular basis, but as far as the physical and mental energy required for teaching goes, what would be my tips there? When Suzy Eddie Izzard decided she was going to run back-to-back marathons, I think she did 20, over 25 days with literally no preparation at all. Yet she was able to go out and run a marathon every day. It sounds extraordinary, but that must be within the scope of an average human being. If you were a refugee and somebody said to you "right, you've got to walk 200 miles in the next 36 hours" or something, you'd probably do it; you wouldn't sleep, you'd just keep going if there was no other choice. And it shows our abilities to do things which we think are extraordinary. That's how I look at my physical health.

If I'm going to the gym, I will always plan three different sorts of sessions, based on the heart rate. I'll put maximum effort in on one, moderate effort on another and very low effort into the other. I measure it, writing down what I've done each session. If I'm not feeling motivated one day, I just look at my book and it makes me want to perform a little better. Within five minutes, you're doing better, and your body adapts, whether you want to or not. The next week you're going to be better still. It's inevitable and it makes things far easier and far more motivating. The next problem is time. At one point I decided I was going to row marathons on the indoor rower and the only training available was written by running coaches. You build up the distance and you end up running 20 miles, but it takes forever. I decided I didn't have time for that and I was going to halve my training time. With interval training, (which is now popularised as HIIT workouts), you spend less time but get more benefit. Again, I wrote it down so I could measure it and then did my final assessment, that marathon row. Incidentally, I came 106th in the world! But the goal is just to measure my improvement. I'm not going to have a target at the end of it where I want to get to, so I haven't got a strength level or body weight I need to reach. I've just got that feeling that every week that I'm going to go to the gym, and I know I'm going to be better because I'm measuring it and I've planned out easy, moderate and difficult sessions.

With lessons, my thinking goes like this: every lesson should be easy. I've got all my planning done because well, hopefully my department's done it, so every lesson is 100% planned. Some senior leadership teams and some heads of department hate this because they walk around and they say, "That teacher, they only spent three minutes looking at that lesson before they delivered it. How are they earning their money? Are they adapting it to their classroom?" And my reply would be "That's the sign of a brilliant curriculum. If someone can just deliver it after three minutes, you will see them adapt it if they're using cold call at random because there are six students they don't know, who don't know the answer. So, they stop the lesson and reteach that point with the visualiser ("Oh, this is what my kids have understood. This is what they haven't understood. I'll adapt in the moment"). You cannot plan for either of those things. You don't know what the kids won't be able to do until you get there in the room, and that's where you earn your money as a teacher.

If you are a teacher in that position, the solution is to turn all your planning into booklets. I wouldn't teach anything without a booklet now, and I would only use a PowerPoint where I need images or videos. The advantage of the booklet is that you've planned exactly the sequence, the resources and the models. You can deviate from that by putting some extras in if you want to. What drives me utterly insane is the number of departments that have a different PowerPoint for each lesson; it's impossible to say, "This links to what we did two weeks ago", but with a booklet we can say, "Let's turn back to page 10." As the booklet is in Word, you can easily display it live on your screen and you can type into it, e.g. "This is where I want you to write. This is my model. This is what I want. Let's do one together". Next time you teach that unit, you now have a model already written to add in. Having everything in a booklet is a massive superpower and if any teachers aren't teaching from booklets, they're shooting themselves in the foot.

GP

Since leaving my first school, I have really been able to find the best parts of the job. I've boiled it down to the following points:

- To do lists are your friend.

- Take the work emails off your devices on holidays, even have an 'out of office' if that helps with anxiety.

- Be honest with students and parents about when you are on holiday or if you're having a weekend off.

- Working on a weekday evening should be for issues of urgency, be irregular or for own personal gain.

- File emails, only keep ones in your inbox that you know you need to deal with.

- Do not sacrifice memories or adventures for excessive work - you're unlikely to get thanked for it.

- Tell your line manager how you achieve work life balance and also if you're ever struggling.

- "Don't smile until Christmas" when you start at a new school is not the greatest advice because students need to see your humanity and personality if you can't have a sense of humour.

- If you don't know the answer then admit it straight away, learn with them, show them you're fallible. If I don't know, I genuinely say so. As I progress further in my career, I just don't have the capacity to know absolutely everything and it's too exhausting to pretend! Just say you're not sure and learn it together.

- Don't go over the top during observations - students see through this and will probably share with your observer. Be consistent, but dynamic.

- It's important to have a network - these might be in your department, it could be just your fellow teachers that started with you, it could be from your previous school.

- I know it will take time but getting a line manager that is a coach rather than dictatorial is a great key to success, try and foster that relationship with them. This has been present in nearly all my schools and I would always want to be the same for those I line manage.

- Teach your students about how you mark and find ways to reduce time by using shorthand, codes, lines and ticks that encourages them to engage in the marking rather than focus on the grade and file the work.

- Don't share workplace frustrations too quickly in new schools; work out the dynamics and relationships to ensure you're not making the situation worse.

You are the most valuable resource in the classroom, take care of it!

SEC

Another thing that interests me, is how responsive the students are to video - and how oddly resistant some schools are to allowing that to be part of the mechanism. So, you can do it in film studies. You can do it to a certain extent, watching Shakespeare plays or whatever. But there are lots of videos that are really supportive. I found that showing those videos and then talking about how the language is applied here or how the dramatic impact happens: it works because they've got a visual now, and it's how they're used to operating, but there's still resistance in a lot of schools. They view it as lazy teaching, I think, but it isn't. It's giving them a different modality to experience and you're only picking specific videos for them to watch, and then you're including that in your greater scheme, aren't you? With students who are easily bored or distracted, you need to hit their 10-minute window of attention, or you don't get their engagement.

I think some of them are extremely grateful to be back after the Covid lockdowns because they needed the support that the school and the peer groups offered them. I think some of them haven't come back. I would say their resilience has improved. I think when they first started coming back, they didn't see the point of, or need for school (particularly those students who were perhaps less socially interactive) but I think their resilience has got a bit better now. It's not resilience in attending, it's resilience in seeing tasks through to the end that I think is still the problem. That covers some lack of self-control and lack of self-starting which they lost. We're going to have to build that back.

I suppose one of my peculiar skills is being able to bring in what they're going to do after school as a perspective to motivate and engage students. It works particularly well in health and social care, but I had an example in English not long ago with a boy whose behaviour was difficult to manage. We have a big farming community and we have at least two or three of these students a year who do this: "There's no point in me learning this. I don't need this because I'm going to drive tractors on the farm," and the parents said he didn't need to read. So I talked to him about the necessity for deciphering all of the documents if he wanted to transport any of his animals and how he was going to read the complex information that came in from the ministry and he had never thought about that but it made him think about things a bit differently. But it takes up so much time in a group of 32 students to get to know them all individually and ask those questions and actively listen to what students (or staff, for that matter) are saying, not formulating your assumptions, your responses, your excuses or your defence before you've heard what someone is going to say.

Even right at the very end of my career now, when we do student feedback forms, which are anonymous and open-ended, they will make observations where you know which teacher it is. That happened to me recently for a shared class where students said they would have preferred me to do what Mrs X does, which is explain it all first, then give it in more detail and then get them to write it up because what I was doing is explaining, then getting them to research it and then write it up and they didn't like the research bit. Now that was an interesting conundrum. I realised that I needed a combination of the two approaches. Once I had adopted that, it felt much more like the other teacher's operation, and they felt more comfortable because I had listened to what they said.

I had caring responsibilities for my mother and both my daughters were extremely ill. The school was phenomenal, unbelievably good at how it handled that. The decision I've made in order to manage the stress is not to sweat the small stuff. There are things I just look at and think, "I'm not doing that because if it's important someone will ask me again." I'm also leaving work earlier.

I'm pretty good at marking now and I would say that there has been a conscious effort to reduce the marking load here. As for the planning: we're now using standardised forms for each key stage, which I think is really supporting new teachers because they don't have time to do this and to have a full understanding, because it's all been planned. But there's no opportunity then to learn how to plan individually with your own ideas and creativity, and that's what I think is going to be a loss to teaching.

We use a lot of visualisers and modelling. That enables us to judge what the baseline learning is in the class and give on-the-spot verbal feedback that's clear and efficient. I'm fortunate because I work in a computer room so I can look at what they're doing and call them out if they're not doing it. Obviously, that doesn't help when they're writing in books, but for that, the visualiser I think has been the best thing in terms of teaching students how to think and can incorporate it into the 'I do, we do, you do.'

However, I wouldn't do away with the PowerPoint slides altogether. I have used them when I've had students that have been unwell (e.g., work from slides 10 to 22, etc.). Also, particularly for those new entry teachers because they have a level of security and understanding of what is required.

What are the fundamentals? Understand the specification and the requirements of the specification as your starting point, because if you don't, you then don't know how to write those circular plans that get your students to where you know they need to be. Actively listen to student conversations in the classroom, so that you can get to know the individual likes and dislikes of the students; so that you can help inspire them by relating what you're teaching directly to their own lived experiences.

Don't miss deadlines if they are fundamentally important to the operation of the school, like tracking deadlines or deadlines that mean somebody else can't do their job if you haven't. But do question whether the order of what you're doing things in is really the order that they need to be done in, or if they even need to be done at all. Don't volunteer for everything - just those things that you have a strong skill set in.

Just working endless hours doesn't make you a better teacher. Plan where you know the hot spots are going to be to make sure you are not loading yourself up with anything else outside socially and warn people around you in advance. This fortnight, for example, don't expect anything out of me socially, because I have all the coursework to be done to get to moderation. I will be exhausted, because the students will all give their coursework to you at the last possible minute!

Use your listening ears. That leads me to the last thing which is: if you can be a mentor, be one, because it constantly renews the way that you're looking at the practice and the older you get and the younger your trainees get, it keeps your pedagogical thinking up to date as well. And you are aware of what those issues are that the younger, less experienced teachers are having to face and then support them in it quietly and inoffensively with just the odd look, when you go into a classroom. When you're building them, you don't even recognise the skills for what they are. Do you remember how it felt when you first went into a classroom to observe? You didn't realise why the teacher was doing what they were doing, and you thought: "Why is that teacher going up to that kid and talking really quietly into that ear or why are they doing something different with another kid?" You didn't understand any of it. You just thought, "I'll go in and disseminate the information." But once you've done it for a time you think, "Oh yes, that's what they're doing," because experienced teachers have an armoury of techniques, those teachers must be making millions and millions of decisions a day about how to respond to each situation, all the time.

Vivienne's VIEWPOINT

Continue to be reflective in your practice. Teaching is a continuous learning curve, especially in the first few years. Stay open to new approaches, flexible enough to adapt and willing to listen to your students. The classroom environment should feel safe, inclusive, and engaging for pupils. Make learning relevant to them and ensure that children understand, not just hear, the lesson. Building strong relationships with parents can improve learning and progress.

Reflection
QUESTIONS

1. What steps can you take to ensure your classroom is a safe and supportive environment for all students?

   _____

   _____

   _____

   _____

2. How do you ensure your lessons are meaningful and relevant to your students?

   _____

   _____

   _____

   _____

3. How can you build more effective communication with parents?

   _____

_____

_____

_____

4. How can you maintain your individuality as a teacher while still aligning with school values?

_____

_____

_____

_____

CHAPTER NINE
WHAT TO HOLD ON TO

Vivienne's **VIEWPOINT**

Today a shy student handed me a little note, which read, "You are a really good teacher and I really enjoy our lessons. You're really nice and understanding and so good at creative writing. I feel my writing has really improved; I definitely think more about punctuation."

One of my favourite leaving cards says, "The years I've spent with you have been absolutely amazing and I'm so grateful for having you. You've been our hilarious, arty and wonderful teacher. Thank you for being part of my story."

Other teachers won't always notice or acknowledge your efforts but when a student does, it means the world to me. If you haven't started a collection yet, make sure you file all these messages somewhere and let them light those dark days when everything feels like a struggle.

GP

It will not be easy, it's not supposed to be; be determined and thorough and remember why you chose to become that teacher.

DS

If you treat the job as an eight-to-five, that's more than most people in the country are working. And we don't have the opportunity to work from home any days in a week. If you stop work at five, would anybody sack you? The answer is no. Absolutely, 100% not. You don't owe your school your body and soul. You owe your school to turn up every day and do the work, and eight-til-five is enough. Make your work fit the eight-to-five and that is it. And don't feel any guilt. Otherwise, you develop the habit, which then becomes really hard to break and there's a contagion in schools of a kind of martyrdom. Two of your friends in your department are working till seven p.m., so you automatically do the same. Your job is to kind of be the influential leader, where they're going to look at you and think: Crikey, she's finished at five, whereas I work until seven... So don't do the overtime!

LOD

If you feel close to burnt out, I advise taking time off if you really need to and not feeling guilty about it, because you're entitled to do so if you log it as stress. Often your GP will be sympathetic about it. Towards the end of it, I was feeling physically sick in the morning before going to work and it's not worth putting your body through that. Also: this is terrible advice, but: care a bit less. Take the pressure off yourself however you can afford it, whether it be not marking the books as well as you normally do, or not taking the books home at all or missing a deadline. It really does also depend on who your manager is as to whether that's feasible.

EP

If I just wanted to teach my subject, I'd go and work at university. I mean, I'd be paid peanuts there as well, but if all I wanted to do is nerd out about English, I could do that elsewhere. The job is: we teach young people and we're teaching them how to 'people', as well as how to write and reason and all the rest of it. That's the important thing.

SG

What keeps me in the profession is the kids. Today when I told them about the exams, I told them "You are not just a number - you have to look at the bigger picture and I know that all of you will be able to actually understand what's going on in conversation in France because there is life after school." There wasn't a sound in the room, but I could see it in their eyes. They got me and they were inspired. I was making a difference at that exact moment. This is why I do this job.

I had this really grown-up conversation with a Year 11, who asked me why I'm a teacher. I replied that Plato used to say immortality exists in two ways - either by having children or through your thoughts and what you teach to others. Plato himself left all his books, his ideas, his philosophical teachings, things we are still referring to 2,000 years later. When you are a teacher, you become immortal in a way because you are passing on something. It might sound a bit arrogant, but the idea of leaving a legacy helps me to stay in the job. What I do will live on in some way.

Reflection QUESTIONS

Teaching is challenging, but staying connected to your reasons for becoming a teacher will keep you motivated. Treat teaching as a job with reasonable hours and boundaries. Rest if you're overwhelmed – your health comes first. Teaching is about making connections, inspiring, and shaping students as individuals - not just delivering subject content. Recognise the lasting impact of your teaching; your influence extends far beyond the classroom.

1. How can you remind yourself regularly of the reasons you chose to become a teacher?

   _____

   _____

   _____

   _____

2. How can you better manage your time to ensure work stays within set hours without sacrificing quality?

   _____

   _____

   _____

   _____

3. What signs of burnout should you look out for, and how can you proactively address them?

   _____

   _____

   _____

   _____

4. How can you create more meaningful moments in your teaching that inspire your students?

   _____

   _____

   _____

   _____

CHAPTER TEN
WHAT CAN YOU DO RIGHT NOW?

For me, perhaps the most important tips to take away from this book
are the following:

- Be fair, kind and consistent to manage behaviour better.
- Sleep, hydration, healthy nutrition and physical activity help
  boost your stamina and mood.
- Identify a mentor inside school and maintain friendships
  outside school.
- Prioritise self-care to protect your mental health and avoid
  overwhelm.
- Consider what you want your legacy to be.
- It's true that what we teachers do is valuable and worthwhile
  and makes a positive difference to young people's lives.

However, there are days when we need to remember that it's only a
job and there is life beyond teaching!

My vision for you after reading this book is that you choose **today** to take back the power to imagine and create a better, more fulfilled work life and a better, more balanced home life (because that's important too).

What I *don't* want you to do is to lose that joy in your imagination and creativity. What I *also* don't want you to do is to lose that feeling that you are in control (not merely going through the motions). Often, when you are in a position of extreme tiredness – body and soul – you can feel overwhelmed and disillusioned by everything. The imagination tends – if not to die, then at least to shrink to a very, very small part of your inner life. So now is the time to start using it again.

If you do nothing else, these are the **five key steps to take now:**

1. Put aside any day-to-day concerns for the moment and think back to **what prompted you to choose teaching as a profession.** Write this down below and take a moment to reflect, without judging your present-day self. **Do you still feel that same sense of purpose?** Add your thoughts on paper.

_____

_____

_____

_____

_____

_____

_____

2. **Do you still feel that same passion for what you do?** Have your priorities changed? What aspect of your job currently fuels your enthusiasm? You don't need to act on any of these thoughts and feelings yet, but you do owe it to yourself to be totally honest and write your thoughts down below.

_____

_____

_____

_____

_____

_____

_____

_____

3. **Go through the following visualisation process:**

Find a quiet space where you won't be disturbed for the next few minutes because I want you to imagine what your future could be like. What can you see? Who can you see around you? Are you at the same school? What does your classroom look like? How do you feel as you walk in, or greet your students? What does it feel like when you see your colleagues after a weekend or half term? What are the qualities of your interactions? Do they leave you feeling optimistic and cheerful? How do you feel at the end of the day? Are you reflective? Are you celebrating the things that went well, the progress of an individual or even the whole class? Perhaps there have just been a couple of students who have made the connections, who now have new ideas that you've sparked...

Or maybe when you look forward to next year or a few years' time, you see yourself in a different setting altogether? Perhaps you're still teaching. I hope you are, because I know you went into teaching with passion and a definite purpose, but maybe you're teaching a different age group, smaller or bigger groups or even 1:1. You could even be standing on a stage at a conference, sharing your ideas with others or gaining new focus and skills and a new perspective.

If you take the time to do this, it can be very powerful. You've heard the well-known saying that whatever you conceive and believe, you can achieve. Make sure that your future is the best possible one you can currently imagine, whether that's pulling up and parking in the staff car park at school with a sense of happy anticipation, or throwing everything up in the air and making a decision to change everything, even the future you thought you'd chosen.

Don't edit anything yet, just write down everything that came into your head, even (or perhaps *especially*) if it surprised you.

_____

_____

4. **You are not *just* a teacher, you're so much *more* than that.** Write down below all the other things that define you as a person beyond your job as a teacher (e.g. I am also a mother, daughter, sister, friend, artist, writer, explorer, chef…)

_____

_____

_____

_____

_____

_____

_____

5. Lastly, list your numerous transferable skills below.

_____

_____

_____

_____

_____

_____

_____

Look back over what you've written and be proud of all you've achieved and all that you are still capable of creating. Now you are armed with all that information (to quote Mary Oliver): *Tell me, what is it you plan to do with your one wild and precious life?*

ABOUT VIVIENNE

As a child I dreamt of writing and illustrating books. Having completed my BA degree in graphic design and tons of private art commissions, I became an image consultant, working with individual and corporate clients to express their personality and feel more confident through personal presentation. My dream of becoming an author came unexpectedly true when my husband upped and left me with a three-week-old baby and a three-year-old. My experiences inspired me to write (and illustrate) my self-help book – 'The Single Mum's Survival Guide' in 2014. I had qualified two years prior to this as a transformational life coach, NLP (Neuro Linguistic Programming) and Ericksonian (from the methods of Carl Erickson) hypnotherapy practitioner. I put this to good use by working with single mums to recover from the trauma of separation, improve their communication with their ex for the children's sake and thrive whilst doing the tough job of solo parenting.

After volunteering to give art classes to my sons' primary school, I became Artist in Residence and also ran an after-school art club from my home studio. Much as I loved this, it wasn't really a viable career, so I studied for my TEFL (Teaching English as a Foreign Language) and TESOL (Teaching English to Speakers of Other Languages) qualifications and spent the next 12 years teaching English to students from a wide range of age groups and nationalities.

TESOL teaching tends to be seasonal, so I added the role of regional director of a women's business networking club, helping my members to build confidence in presenting and marketing their businesses. During this period, I presented the Business show on a not-for-profit radio station, interviewing local business owners and encouraging them to share their stories with the local community.

In 2019 I had a bit of a revelation when I realised that whatever I've done in my career, I've always been drawn to training or teaching so I bit the bullet, sold my networking franchise and – now over 50 years old, enrolled at University for my master's level PGCE (Post Graduate Certificate in Education) in secondary English.

Today I work as an oracy leader for a charity called the English Speaking Union, helping young people to discover their voice through public speaking and debating workshops. I also work with teachers in CPD (Continuing Professional Development) sessions exploring how to embed oracy into the curriculum (both learning to talk and learning through talk) as a whole-school approach.

For part of the week, I work as a 1:1 English teacher, with private clients as well as students who attend a wonderful alternative learning provision centre nearby. Tailoring my teaching to the needs of the individual pupil is so rewarding.

I also find I am using my coaching skills with an increasing number of pupils to help them combat stress and overwhelm and build confidence. The same could be said of the teachers I work with now – always online and 1:1 and at times that suit them, whether that's during half term or the holidays. It means so much to me to be able to act as a catalyst of positive change in the lives of teachers who so often put their own peace of mind and wellbeing behind everyone else's.

WORKING WITH VIVIENNE

If you want to delve deeper into any of the ideas explored in this book, I work individually with teachers to help them rediscover their passion and purpose and arrive at a place where they feel positive and resourceful, whether they choose to leave or stay within the profession. Everyone needs a safe and non-judgemental space to tell their teaching story, a kind mirror to reflect back patterns of thoughts and behaviours that are holding them back from achieving the life they deserve; some people need a springboard to allow them to reach the best decision about their career and most people need time to reflect and consider their next best steps with a helpful guide at their side, who will support them no matter what, helping them to achieve greater clarity along the way.

My coaching packages consist of six hours, to be taken at a time and pace that suits you. I offer slots during half terms and holidays because that is when you are likely to have the time and headspace to glean the most benefit from your sessions.

If you own a copy of this book, you are entitled to a special discount price on your coaching package. I also have helpful free resources to assist you in making that transition away from being a tired teacher and keep you feeling purposeful, clear and energised on a daily basis whilst achieving your goals in your professional and personal life.

Please email me at hello@vivienne-smith.co.uk with 'coaching and resources' as your subject heading to find out more. Book your free, no-obligation discovery call with me here: